SIMPLE SENTE[NCES]

N V	Bob plays. / ⟶ /	N V
	Bob is playing. / ⟶ /	
N V A	Bob arrives hungry. / ⟶ /	N V A
N V Ad	Bob plays well. / ⟶ /	N V Ad
	Bob plays on the team. / ⟶ /	
N V N	Bob plays ball. / ⟶ /	N V N
N V N N	Bob calls his dog Spot. / ⟶ /	N V N N
N V N N	Bob gives his dog milk. / ⟶ /	N V N N
N Lv N	Bob is a boy. / ⟶ /	N Lv N
N Lv A	Bob is strong. / ⟶ /	N Lv A
N Lv Ad	Bob is here. / ⟶ /	N Lv Ad
	Bob is in the house. / ⟶ /	

ELEMENTS OF INTONATION PATTERNS

4 stresses	4 pitch levels	4 junctures and terminals
/ ∧ \ ᵕ	l n h hh	/ + / / ⟶ / / ⟋ / / ⟶ /

Linguistics
and the
Teaching of Reading

CURRICULUM AND METHODS IN EDUCATION

ARNO A. BELLACK, *Consulting Editor*

Carl A. Lefevre

Professor of English
Chicago Teachers College North

McGraw-Hill Book Company

New York   San Francisco   Toronto   London

*Linguistics
and the
Teaching of Reading*

Linguistics and the Teaching of Reading

Library of Congress Catalog Card Number 63-13143

37020

Preface

This volume presents a basic exploration of the contribution that twentieth-century language scholarship can make to teaching the skills of literacy—reading and writing, the first two of the three R's. It is intended to have a broad appeal to parents and other laymen as well as students and teachers.

The method proposed in this book is a whole-sentence method that applies a scientific description of American English utterances to the problems of teaching reading. No one can get meaning from the printed page without taking in whole language patterns at the sentence level, because these are the minimal meaning-bearing structures of most written communications. While this ability in itself is no warranty of success in reading, it is a minimum requirement. The new and distinctive feature of this sentence method is the application of a modern linguistic description of speech patterns to their graphic counterparts, or equivalent patterns in writing and print. Also included is more accurate information on the relationships of basic sounds and letters (spelling) than is provided in most phonics systems. Although the linguistic materials are steadily focused throughout the book on reading and the teaching of reading, the same approach is applicable to the different but related problems of writing.

In both style and content the Introduction is quite different from the text proper. Because it summarizes important theoretical framework and linguistic detail, the Introduction is concentrated and proceeds by straight-line exposition; its pages are numbered as preliminary matter. Grasp of the basic points covered in this Introduction is required for any rigorous understanding of descriptive linguistics and structural grammar. Readers who prefer to get into the more practical discussion of applications first, however, may choose to skip the Introduction and return to it when they have read the book.

Beginning with Chapter 1 and continuing to the end, this book is not written in textbook style. It is meant to be readable and persuasive. I hope it sounds alive and interesting. Presentation of certain technical points goes by a kind of incremental repetition rather than by the straight-line expository method of the Introduction. Sometimes a restatement may have value as a simple reminder of an important point, or as a reminder in a new context; or a statement may acquire a new value because the reader's understanding has reached a higher level.

This volume as a whole is designed to provide an accessible introduction to modern linguistics and some of its applications to teaching the skills of literacy at all levels; it is designed to provide an essential minimum of information, adequate in linguistic rigor, for this purpose. It may also chance to interest the specialist who has not previously entered its domain.°

° This book is a complete revision of the book entitled *Linguistics and the Teaching of Reading,* copyrighted by the author in January, 1962, and published first in a multilith edition in April, 1962, by the Institute for Educational Theory. The present Preface and Introduction are the outgrowth of reorganization and a complete rewriting of the original Preface, including material previously in

Linguistics and the Teaching of Reading owes a great deal to those scientific language scholars of this century, the descriptive linguists and structural grammarians, some of whose important works are mentioned at the end of the Introduction; more are included in the bibliographical appendix. These scholars are not responsible for any shortcomings, errors, or omissions that may be noted; the author hereby acknowledges his responsibility.

A distillation of many years of teaching, this book inevitably owes much to professional colleagues. It owes perhaps even more to students, especially at Chicago Teachers College North, where over one thousand have studied the multilith trial edition as a basic text in their first college course in English, or in the language arts methods course. The students' tenacity and their pride in collaboration contributed in many ways to rounding out the first edition to the shape of the present one. Unnumbered helpful persons must remain anonymous. Only a few who made special contributions can be cited by name.

Early in 1961, Adrian Sanford helped to focus the original idea of the book; he offered constant encouragement during its shaping and reshaping. Richard S. Rudner's precise insights were uniquely helpful in clarifying the theoretical framework of substantive and methodological assumptions set forth in the Introduction: Contributions to the Theory of Reading. H. A. Gleason, Jr., wrote a detailed critique of the trial edition that influenced

---

the Notes at the end of the book; these two new preliminary sections embody fresh material as well as important revisions. Other extensive revisions, including both new substantive matter and new interpretations, have been made in the following chapters at the heart of the book: Chapter 3. "The Child's Language from Cradle to Kindergarten"; Chapter 4. "Intonation. The Melodies of the Printed Page"; Chapter 5. "Sentence Patterns, Function Order, Word Groups." Chapter 8 has been retitled. Numerous corrections, restatements, and expansions have been incorporated throughout the book in response to suggestions from consultants, colleagues, friends—and as result of working closely with several hundred college students who used the multilith trial edition of the book during three regular semesters. The Notes at the end have also been augmented. Four entirely new sections have been added: a summary of the abbreviations and special symbols used throughout the book; an illustrated description of the human speech apparatus, with reference to the phonemic system of American English; a select bibliography, classified and annotated; and an index of 519 entries.

the present version in important particulars. Finally, and most inadequately, I express my appreciation for the help of Helen Lefevre, my wife and fellow scholar-teacher, who kept the work under scrutiny and made substantive contributions to it.

CARL A. LEFEVRE

Introduction

Basic linguistic theory:
Contributions to a theory of reading

Reading and reading theory are of great practical significance to everyone. Traditional reading methodology, however, does not concern itself *rigorously* with language. Instead, it concerns itself largely with psychological problems, with visual perception especially. The question is, visual perception of what, exactly, if not of the graphic counterparts in printed form of meaning-bearing language patterns? To comprehend printed matter, the reader must perceive entire language structures as wholes—as unitary meaning-bearing patterns. Short of this level of perception, the reader simply does not perceive those total language structures that alone are capable of carrying meaning. He may perceive individual words as if words were meaning-bearing units in themselves, one of the most serious of all reading disabilities. Or he may group words visually in structureless pattern-fragments that do not and cannot bear meaning. What such readers do not do is read total language patterns for total comprehension of meaning. My basic assumption is that reading must be regarded as a language-related process; reading and the teaching of reading must therefore be rigorously studied in relation to language. Today, rigorous study of language means structural linguistics.

Current reading methods and materials reflect little or no acquaintance with the structural linguistic rationale. This scientific basis of twentieth-century advancement in language scholarship was foreshadowed in Sapir's *Language* (1921) and then catalyzed in 1933 by Bloomfield's *Language.* This is thirty to forty years ago now. Since 1933, the scientific study of languages, including American English, has laid the foundation for a new approach to language learning, both native and foreign. In essence, structural linguistics is cultural-anthropological: language is studied objectively and systematically as a learned arbitrary code of vocal symbols through which men in a given culture communicate with each other, interact, and cooperate.

It makes little difference whether a language has an ancient and honorable tradition of literacy, or is simply the speech of a people who have never developed a writing system. Language is viewed as a vocal symbol-system from which a graphic symbol-system may or may not have been derived. Handwriting and print are seen as secondary, derivative codes of visual symbols that reflect the basic language learned before formal schooling begins. This is a position of far-reaching consequences for education, pointing toward new theories of language learning and teaching, new methods, and new materials.

But linguists and linguistics cannot do this vital educational work by themselves. Professionally qualified, experienced teachers must study linguistics and discover for themselves how to apply new knowledge and new insights to old problems. Teachers must teach themselves and they must teach the teachers—teachers in service and teachers in preparation—for a more effective attack on the development of literacy in our schools. This whole range of activity is the professional concern of teaching, not of linguistics. It is also the concern of parents, and of all citizens who take an active interest in education. Few linguists are capable and experienced as English or language arts teachers; and technical linguists have many problems of their own, still to be solved. In the meantime, linguistics has a very great deal to offer that is sorely needed; the results of linguistic science are there for the taking. Reading instruction should make full use of this new knowledge.

As for myself, I am primarily a humanist rather than a linguistic scientist, though I do not feel that science is alien to the humanities. On the contrary, science is one of the humanities— or should be. As a scholar-teacher of English, I have made it my professional business to apply relevant findings of structural linguistics in teaching language and literature to students of all ages. I have also tried to determine just what and how much linguistic knowledge of English is needed by persons who introduce the young to the basic skills of literacy. In language arts methods and other college English courses I have made it a point to integrate linguistic knowledge with the more traditional subject matter. Structural linguistics can enrich as well as clarify many areas of the language arts.

This book presents the basic linguistic knowledge of English that my experience suggests is needed by persons who introduce the young to literacy—parents as well as teachers. My purpose throughout has been to explain English speech in relation to reading as simply and clearly as possible, without compromising the rigor of the underlying linguistic principles and data.

This book is intended for all who have a part in developing literacy in the young: school, college, and university teachers; of English language and literature, of language arts methods, and of reading; students preparing to teach, in-service teachers; school administrators, program supervisors, curriculum specialists; parents, relatives, and friends of children. It is a basic work on reading.

A number of broad substantive and methodological assumptions underlie this linguistic approach to a theory of reading. Two basic substantive assumptions are as follows:

1. Language is human behavior.

2. Each language has its own independent and unique structure; it requires its own independent and unique description. This structure or system, taken as a whole, is the grammar of the language.

Four basic methodological assumptions are as follows:

1. Language may be studied objectively and systematically.

2. Objective study of a language yields an accurate, orderly, comprehensive description of the language system, or structure.

3. Structural linguistics is not just another nomenclature for "the parts of speech" of traditional grammar, or another way of parsing and diagramming sentences. It is an entirely new way of looking at language, of sorting out the data, of classifying findings.

4. Structural linguistics leads to new data, new knowledge, new insights, new understandings.

Such broad substantive and methodological assumptions have illuminated my classroom experience as a teacher of literature and the skills of literacy—*and as a teacher of teachers.* They have led me to close study of basic linguistic principles and data, and eventually to the view of reading summarized in this Introduction and developed at length in the whole book.

Precise linguistic principles are embodied in the basic Trager-Smith system of language analysis at three levels: (1) phonemes, (2) morphemes, and (3) syntax. Familiarity with this analysis, though not required of the reader, is implicit in much of the discussion.[1] *

1. *Phonemes.* Phonemes are the basic sound units of language. A phoneme is the smallest class of significant speech sounds. The "segmental" phonemes are the nine simple vowels, the three semivowels and the twenty-one consonants of American English. The nine simple vowel phonemes are the short vowels of traditional terminology. The long vowels are not described by linguists as phonemes because every long vowel sound is composed of one simple vowel phoneme followed by one semivowel phoneme.

* All notes are at the end of the book, beginning page 199.

The technical term for such a combination of two phonemes is *complex vowel nucleus*. The vowel sounds in the words *grow* and *trees* are examples of long vowels, or complex vowel nuclei. Since long vowels are not phonemes, they are not represented in the phonemic alphabet. Unlike the Roman alphabet we use in English writing and print, the phonemic alphabet uses one symbol and only one symbol for one phoneme. The phonemic alphabet does use many of the letters of the Roman alphabet but adds special phonemic symbols to carry out the principle of one symbol, one phoneme. Each symbol in the phonemic alphabet stands for one basic speech sound in the language system. The phonemic alphabet makes possible linguistically accurate transcriptions of American English speech and all its dialects.

In addition to the segmental vowel and consonant phonemes, Trager and Smith also designate as phonemes four levels of pitch, four degrees of stress on syllables, and four junctures or ways of terminating the speech stream. These twelve phonemes of American English speech have special linguistic significance in the system or code of audio-lingual signals. In contradistinction to the thirty-three segmental phonemes, the twelve phonemes of pitch, stress, and juncture may be thought of as nonsegmental phonemes. The total number of phonemes is thus forty-five. In my approach to the language and to reading, I treat the twelve significant features of pitch, stress, and juncture under the heading of intonation.

2. *Morphemes.* Morphemes are the basic meaning-bearing units of language. A morpheme is an indivisible language element patterned out of phonemes. Morphemes include word bases (roots), prefixes, suffixes, and word-form changes, or inflections. A free morpheme may pattern by itself in larger language structures; a bound morpheme must combine with another morpheme. Such single words as *cat, go,* and *black* are examples of free morphemes; *pro-* and *-tect* in *protect* are examples of bound morphemes.

3. *Syntax.* Syntax includes the various patternings of morphemes into larger structural units: noun groups, verb groups, noun clusters, verb clusters, prepositional groups, clauses, and sentences.

Moreover, sentence-level utterances in American English make use of four signaling systems. These four signaling systems, in descending order of importance are, as I see them: (1) intonation, (2) syntactical-function order in sentence patterns, (3) structure words, and (4) word-form changes.

1. *Intonation.* Intonation is the generic term for significant and distinctive patterns of pitch, stress, and juncture. Comprising intricate patterns of obligatory and optional features, intonation is perhaps the least understood signaling system of American English. It has been intensively studied for no more than two decades.

2. *Syntactical-function order in sentence patterns.* There are possibly no more than four important sentence patterns in American English. Variety is achieved through nearly endless possibilities of expansion, substitution, inversion, and transformation of these important patterns.

3. *Structure words.* About three hundred "empty" words, having few referents outside the language system itself, and relatively lacking in meaning or content; contrasted to "full" words having referents in the real world outside language. Structure words include many sets, such as noun markers, verb markers, phrase markers, clause markers, question markers, and sentence connectors.

4. *Word-form changes* (grammatical inflections, prefixes, and suffixes). Word-form changes include noun plurals, possessives, verb parts, adjective comparison, and the like, as well as derivational prefixes and suffixes. Word-form changes include most of the bound morphemes.

I make explicit use of the three levels of language analysis and of the four signaling systems in my explanation of the interactions of speech and reading.

Beyond reading readiness, six methods of basic reading instruction that relate to language analysis have been traditionally suggested. Usually a sort of warning is added to the effect that an "eclectic," or "multilinear," method is best. "There is no one method of teaching reading" is the motto, or slogan. The terms *alphabet, phonic, word, phrase, sentence,* and *story* methods seem to refer to categories of language or discourse; but so far as the eclectic, or multilinear, method has not proved either eclectic or multilinear enough to include an accurate description of our language structure. Actually, all six of these so-called methods attempt to reach meaning virtually without analysis of meaning-bearing language structures.

Discussions of reading methodology abound with such expressions as *fused thought content, eye span, meaning units, fusing single words into sequences of meaning,* and so on. The missing part in all these explanations is simply the meaning-bearing structural patterns of American English. It is almost as though meaning could be reached by visual perception of graphic symbols unrelated to the structure of the language they represent.[2]

Current reading methodology, so far as it concerns itself with language at all, in fact focuses on letters and words as the most significant units. This narrow limitation holds true even of the several linguistic treatments of reading that limit themselves largely to basic sounds and spelling. All are based in whole or in part on the original suggestions made by Bloomfield about twenty years ago, before structural linguistics had developed modern descriptions of English syntax. These linguistic applications substantially accept the traditional phonics approach to reading instruction, but within this narrow limitation they do provide accurate information on sound-spelling relationships in English. The main concern is still the single word.

On the other hand, in my approach to reading instruction, the word is treated as a minor language unit for many reasons. Some of these reasons are linguistic, others are pedagogical. In English the word is an unstable element, whether it is taken as a semantic or as a structural unit. The most significant structures in English are intonation patterns, grammatical and syntactical word groups, clauses, and sentences.

Single words, analyzed and spoken in isolation, assume the intonation contours of whole utterances. Single words thus lose the characteristic pitch and stress they normally carry in the *larger constructions that comprise the flow of speech and bear meaning.* This automatic upgrading of words may lead many learners to "read" word by word, or by pattern fragments, without regard for whole structural patterns that carry meaning. This upgrading may thus contribute to the frequency and extent of serious reading disability among pupils of all ages. So far, little has been done to develop reading of American English by its known structures instead of by its vocabulary.

What is proposed here is a new sentence method of teaching reading, applying a linguistic description of American English utterances at the sentence level to their graphic counterparts, written and printed sentences. Such a structural linguistic approach to reading and to reading instruction appears very promising, and there is some experimental evidence to support it.[3]

Like any explication of basic theory, the present one has an immediate context that helps locate and define it. Five important elements of this context may be stated as follows:

1. Not enough is known about why some students learn to read while others do not. In particular, not enough is known about why many bright children do not learn to read well.

2. Reading ability does not correlate reliably with intelligence, nor with any other measurable human trait.

3. Profound confusion prevails in English teaching and in language arts instruction generally over the relationship of reading and writing to speech. Educated but linguistically unsophisticated persons tend to regard the graphic system as the norm for both speech and writing.

4. Lacking a rigorous theoretical base, the so-called eclectic, or multilinear, theory of reading instruction and of the multiple causation of reading failures begs many questions and tends to avoid the responsibility for solutions.

5. Consequently, efforts should be made to develop a reading theory comparable in rigor to theories in other disciplines; structural linguistics can make a major contribution to such a theory.

Within this broad context, the following fourteen substantive assumptions comprise the basis of this approach to reading according to my present understanding. These statements are offered as contributions to a theory of reading and reading instruction.

1. Reading is basically a language-related process.
2. *a.* Language is speech, an arbitrary code or system of vocal symbols. It is noninstinctive behavior; it must be learned.
   b. Graphic symbols of writing and print comprise a secondary, derivative system.
   c. Thus, two interrelated symbol systems interact, the manual-visual with the audio-lingual.
3. *a.* Infants and young children naturally learn language playfully; they enjoy the game and they enjoy themselves as they play it.
   b. This natural spirit of play should be encouraged and developed fully at all levels of language instruction.
4. *a.* Simply by talking, normal children from five to seven years old demonstrate their mastery of the basic structures of American English.
   b. Children should learn to read and write the language they already speak and understand.
5. *a.* Learning a native language is quite different from learning a foreign language. Similarly, developing literacy in the mother tongue is different from learning to read and write a foreign tongue.
   b. Developing literacy in the native language should proceed on the analogy of learning native speech as infant and child.
6. *a.* Graphics—the representation of language in writing and print—is essentially a "shorthand." It is a mnemonic device which can effect recall of entire meaning-bearing language patterns, sentences predominantly.
   b. Efficient reading requires consciousness of the relative equivalency of the graphic counterparts to spoken language structures.
7. Accordingly, some reading problems can be solved by developing consciousness of pertinent language processes and their interrelationships with graphics. This statement applies especially to the relationship of written and printed symbols to their equivalent speech segments.
8. The sentence is not merely a sequence of words, but a unitary meaning-bearing pattern of grammatical and syntactical

functions: the individual words are relatively minor elements in such unitary patterns.

9. *a.* Individual words have less significance to hearer or reader than is commonly attributed to them.

   b. The significant elements are grammatical and syntactical structures: noun and verb groups and clusters, clauses, sentences.

10. Analytical slicing of larger language segments and their graphic counterparts into smaller segments should be done only to the extent that the reading process itself requires it.

11. *a.* The language learner, like any other, learns what he practices. If he practices analyzing, spelling, and "sounding" words and word parts, that is what he will learn. He may learn something else accidentally, or incidentally; and he may not.

    b. The child learning to read should practice reading entire meaning-bearing language patterns at the sentence level.

12. Mastering the graphic system by giving his main attention to larger patterns, a learner would develop his own inductive generalizations or sound-spelling relationships (and this largely through his writing); in reading he would need formal spelling instruction only to get him over difficulties.

13. The American English sentence should be read not as a sequence of words but as a unitary meaning-bearing sequence of structural functions clearly signaled and patterned by (*a*) intonation; (*b*) syntactical functions in basic sentence patterns; (*c*) structure words; and (*d*) word-form changes.

14. In developing literacy in the native language, mutual reinforcement of skills may be achieved by coordinating the teaching of auding, speaking, reading, and writing in the same lessons, so far as practicable.

   (The term *auding* is used here and throughout the book instead of *listening*. *Auding* is needed because it means specifically comprehending and responding appropriately to the patterns of speech. As a term, *auding* is more precise than *listening*, which refers not only to speech patterns but to all sounds, from musical compositions to the merest noise. Moreover, *auding* connotes greater concentration and attentiveness to language patterns and meaning—perhaps sharper intellectual activity than *listening*, which is comparatively passive.)

The view of reading developed in this book is not offered as a "panacea," a defensive epithet used by some reading specialists. It is offered for study and reflection, and as a stimulus to research and experimentation. If this view is deeply and widely considered, I believe it may contribute—qualitatively—to modification and basic improvement in reading theory and instruction. It is time for the field of reading to reflect the great contribution made by twentieth-century language scholars to our understanding of all language processes—and to our understanding of reflective and conceptual thought.*

CARL A. LEFEVRE

* I refer to such well-known linguistic works as Sapir's *Language* (1921), Bloomfield's *Language* (1933), Fries' *American English Grammar* (1940), Bloch and Trager's *Outline of Linguistic Analysis* (1942), Pike's *The Intonation of American English* (1946), Harris' *Methods in Structural Linguistics* (1951), Trager and Smith's *An Outline of English Structure* (1951), Whitehall's *Structural Essentials of English* (1951), Fries' *The Structure of English* (1952), Gleason's *An Introduction to Descriptive Linguistics* (1955), Whorf's *Language, Thought, and Reality* (1956, posthumous), Roberts' *Patterns of English* (1956), Chomsky's *Syntactic Structures* (1957), Francis, *The Structure of American English* (1958), Hill's *Introduction to Linguistic Structures* (1958), Hockett's *A Course in Modern Linguistics* (1958), a volume of reprints from periodicals edited by Allen, *Readings in Applied Linguistics* (1958), E. T. Hall's *The Silent Language* (1959), and a number of books by Brooks, Bryant, Carroll, Marckwardt, Roberts, Sledd, Warfel, and other authors. This is a highly selective list; a complete bibliography of books and articles published in the last thirty to forty years would run to many pages. See the Selected Bibliography at the end of this book for a short list of suggestions for further reading.

Contents

CHAPTER ONE

*A program for applying
structural linguistics
to reading instruction:
a preview and guide
to this book*

Too many children and adults cannot read for personal enjoyment and fulfillment; others cannot read adequately for vocational or professional development. Their inability to read is an obstacle to their attaining full maturity either as citizens or as private persons. Nonreaders are much more than an economic liability; they are deeply wounded human beings. And they are legion in American life.

They exist despite the efforts of thousands of dedicated teachers, despite study of visual perception and psychology of reading, despite a plethora of beautifully printed (and expensive) reading textbooks, basal readers, graded workbooks, and so on. They exist despite the almost universal recognition that in our increasingly automated culture, literacy is of crucial importance. Under modern conditions, national needs greatly increase old demands for literate persons in all occupations and in all walks of life. Chapter 2 presents arresting evidence of the seriousness of the reading problem in America.

Coping with the problems of learning to read will require Americans to bring to bear all relevant and pertinent knowledge, including *modern knowledge of reading as a language-related process*. So far, little linguistic knowledge has been applied in developing reading materials and methodology; what has been applied is largely confined to accurate description of the relationships of sounds to spelling, the subject traditionally known as phonics. While linguistic knowledge of this special topic is clearly superior to much received misinformation, it only hints at the contribution linguistics can make toward a genuine solution of the problems of reading instruction. What more can be done?

The Introduction outlines the general theory underlying my approach to a solution. This chapter and the rest of this book present what I judge to be a necessary minimum of modern language information, insight, and attitude as a basis for a linguistically sound methodology of teaching basic reading skills (interrelated with other language skills), and for remedial teaching at all levels. In no sense is this material to be dismissed as a panacea, guaranteed to solve all our problems overnight. Perhaps there is no solution, either immediate or ultimate, though this seems doubtful. If a solution is to be found, modern knowledge of American English will be crucial to the process of discovery. The purpose of this book is to initiate that process.

The first understanding to be reached in attempting a fresh approach to basic language learnings is that *language is fundamentally and primarily audio-lingual,* a matter of mouth and ear. Writing and printing are based on speech and derived from it; their visual representation of certain aspects of language reminds the ear not only of the sounds of words, but of our native American English intonation, the overall melody and rhythm of entire utterances. Writing and print are thus mnemonic devices whose main function is to effect recall of entire language patterns, sentence-level utterances in particular. True knowledge of reading and writing processes begins with searching study of the interrelationships of language patterns and their graphic counterparts.

To control the graphic system of American English requires that teachers recognize those primary and distinctive elements of the spoken language that are reliably signaled in writing and print. *Primary* and *distinctive* apply to those elements that occur systematically throughout the language and therefore may be explained by the basic sound system, and by grammar and syntax; they are distinct from—in a structural sense they underlie and support—expressions of individual attitude, emphasis, and interpretation. This book largely omits what some linguists call *paralanguage* and *kinesics* (or combine in the term *metalinguistics*), because these elements are largely omitted in graphic representations of language.

Associated with some reading failures, no doubt, are sociological, medical, neurological, psychiatric, psychological, and other conditions—if not as causes, then as effects. Grace M. Fernald, in a valuable earlier book, writes that certain definite physical and psychological conditions are often mistaken for *causes* of reading disability when they may be in fact *by-products* of the disability.[1] *While aware of complex causations, I believe misapprehending the relationships between spoken and printed language patterns—a problem that can be illuminated by lin-*

guistic insights—to be the most decisive element in reading failures. For this reason, this book develops the primary audio-lingual system of the language first, and then relates the secondary and derived manual-graphic system to it.

A word may be in order here about "inner speech." The eye is more fleet than tongue or ear; visual reading can go like the wind, with full comprehension, but only if it takes in whole language patterns in its purview. Functional association of graphic patterns with the audio-lingual processes of larger structures does not entail vocalization, nor such crudities in visual reading failures as mumbling, which is a symptom of word calling, or word-by-word reading. Yet even the most fleeting visual skimming probably carries vestigial traces of inner speech.

The basic fault in poor reading (viewed as a crippled language process) is poor sentence sense, demonstrated orally in word calling, or in reading various nonstructural fragments of language patterns as units; it is not likely that a word caller in oral reading will read silently by language structures. Alphabet and word methods of primary reading instruction naturally tend toward word and fragment reading, especially if the child is not taught to read printed and written segments as graphic counterparts of the larger structures of his language.

The single word in English is by no means a principal language unit. The word is actually a very slippery creature, a chameleon in *both structure and meaning.* For example, a "concrete noun," like *skin,* may be distributed in language patterns in the position of a noun (*snake skin, skin of your teeth*); of a verb (*skin a cat, skin the buyer*); of an adjective (*skin color, skin texture*); or of an adverb (*skin deep, skin tight*). Simple nouns such as *table* and *chair* may mean a great many different things both concrete and abstract, not to mention their other possible functions in language structures. In a sense, each "word" discovers its meaning and use in every sentence where it occurs. Real dangers lurk in dictionary or vocabulary study that over-stresses single words at the expense of structural and meaning-bearing language patterns.

Moreover, single words analyzed out of context and spoken as separate structures cannot help losing their natural sound as the child hears it in the everyday melodies of pitch, stress, and juncture in American English language patterns. Drill on isolated words, removed from their regular positions in larger structures and unavoidably given the intonation of complete utterances, tends toward oral calling of words in series, or toward uttering pointless structural fragments in oral reading. Unhappy children do this in their efforts to read. Word calling may lay a foundation for a parallel word-seeing procedure in silent reading, with no visual grasp of whole language patterns that carry or lead to meaning. Such "reading" is not reading at all, but a mere parroting of words.

This book proposes much greater attention to the larger structural patterns of the child's language in basic reading and writing instruction than has been given in the past; and less to phonics and vocabulary study, which are incidental rather than fundamental to learning to read American English. Children should first be taught to read and write the same language that they already speak and understand when they enter school; childish immaturities should be endured and more mature habits left to normal maturation. The first task of reading instruction should be to give pupils a conscious knowledge of the language patterns they have mastered on the unconscious operational level. Development of this consciousness should be an integral part of instruction in auding, speaking, reading, handwriting, and composition. (The term *auding* is defined in the Introduction, page xx, item 14.) So far as practicable, language lessons should include all aspects of these interrelated language processes in order to achieve maximum mutual reinforcement of skills. Experience charts can be very effective, especially when they are individualized and do not oversimplify the child's language, or seek to standardize it at an infantile level.

Children who are taught to read with main emphasis on larger patterns than words would be expected to develop their own generalizations of spelling-sound relationships (phonics)— adequate for the purposes of reading—by a guided inductive process in the normal course of learning the graphic system. If reading difficulties then arose because some children did not, special instruction could be devised to help them; accurate and up-to-date information for this purpose is provided in Chapter 8. In teaching children to read, we should analytically slice larger language segments into smaller ones only to the extent that the learning process requires it. This is the heart of the approach: moving as needed from larger to smaller wholes.

Aside from general observation, there is specific evidence that children can learn to read well without any separate, formal instruction in word analysis. Mrs. Doris H. Flinton, director of a current reading experiment in Delmar, New York, reports this kind of learning in her work, which stresses the development of sentence sense. "Examples," she writes, "may be found in the significant superiority of the experimental children, both boys and girls, in spelling and composition, and the transfer to new reading materials with vocabularies quite different from those they have learned before." [2]

Fernald's fine but neglected book, instinct with linguistic understanding, reports that *pupils who had never been taught "phonics," words grouped by sounds, or single words except in context, could pass any phonics test up to grade level.*[3] The author reasons that children learn to associate structural and other elements of new words in much the same way as they recognize visual similarities and differences generally in non-verbal experience. Examples of this kind of associational discrimination are telling identical twins apart, or differentiating and naming all the individuals in litters of puppies or kittens, familiar achievements of youngsters the world over.

The system or code of American English, as described by modern language scholars, has a relatively limited structure system; most of it, but not quite all, is controlled by the child when he enters school. For this reason, Chapter 3 presents the development of the child's language from cradle to kindergarten, beginning with his first primordial squall and concluding with reading readiness. This discussion includes the early development of intonation patterns that are fundamental to our language; the early development of phonemes, morphemes, words, word-form changes; and the early development of sentence patterns: statements, requests, questions. Chapter 3 also differentiates grammatical and syntactical intonation patterns from interpretive aspects of intonation in this discussion—the normal, high-frequency, and obligatory from the optional—in order to lay a basis for keeping them distinct throughout the book.

Chapter 4 deals in greater detail with intonation, or, from the point of view of reading, "the melodies of the printed page." Here four important declarative sentence tunes are presented, as well as tunes identifying questions and requests, and several important stress patterns in phrases and word groups. Because of the basic importance of intonation in American English, and the importance of making children conscious of the relation of intonation to reading and writing, Chapter 4 is a comprehensive introductory treatment, augmented and expanded at specific points throughout the book. Since we hear and speak our language all of a piece and all at once, there is no way to present a description of it in a sequence or even a panorama without cross references and flashbacks.

Intonation is the first and most important of the four main language devices that signal and shape the larger patterns of American English: intonation, function order in sentence patterns, structure words, and word-form changes; all four, including important features of intonation, are represented in writing and print—though only partially, because much that we say and hear cannot be represented graphically in ordinary English writing. Since children five to seven years old are already experienced *at an unconscious level* in the basic use of these language signals, basic reading and writing instruction should develop the child's consciousness of them, especially in oral reading. The child must be taught to relate entire speech patterns to their graphic counterparts, that is, to the written or printed equivalents of language patterns that carry meaning. Bridging the gap between language and graphics is the essence of reading American English as a language process.

Every symbol in the graphic systems of writing and print contributes to *the partial representation* of the overall speech melodies, and of the rhythms of stress and juncture. These are the components of intonation. Capital letters, periods, semicolons, question marks; the order and grouping of words and main sentence parts; the use of such structure words as *the, into, because, when,* and scores of others; and the word-form changes signaling number, tense, possession—all these partially represent limited features of intonation; taken all together, they may visually suggest whole meaning-bearing patterns, and remind the ear of their native tunes.

Syntactical intonations, as part of the structure of the language, can be accurately described in terms of pitch, stress, and juncture; emotionally neutral, they are normal, high-frequency, or obligatory for all speakers. At the sentence level, the syntactical intonations of speech find some graphic representation in the distinctive patterns of declarative statements, requests, and questions. Since most native speakers have an unconscious, intuitive control of these intonations in speech, this knowledge should be used to develop sentence sense in reading and writing. Chapters 3 and 4 are designed as a basis for such instruction in comprehension of meaning.

In reading as in speech, a reliable clue to sentence structure is word order, or order of syntactical functions in sentence patterns, discussed in Chapter 5. Despite the great variety of sentences in American English, our basic sentence order is rigid and arbitrary; variety is achieved through subordination, expansion, and substitution within patterns, and through pattern inversions and transformations. Normal sentence order involves the basic functions of subject first, and verb second, and possibly a "completer" third, which may include a direct or indirect object, an object complement, or a noun or adjective complement. These sentence functions may include simple or involved expansion; a great variety of patterns may be achieved by substitution of one structure for another within the functions; requests and questions vary the basic sentence patterns, but in systematic ways. For reading instruction, the order of basic functions in American English sentences is essentially simple; it should be taught to children at the earliest possible time. Pupils who learn it thoroughly will not call out words in pointless series, with no regard to the meanings inherent in structural patterns.

In Chapter 6, "Structure Words," a distinction is made between two quite different kinds of vocabulary: "full" words and "empty" words. Most words are full words, words having specific meanings, such as *apple, run, yellow, spirally;* but the most frequently used words are the relatively few empty words (about three hundred) having chiefly structural meaning, such as *the, up, when, nevertheless.* Full words may generally be grouped into the four form classes, noun, verb, adjective, and adverb—but words are most clearly defined functionally or structurally in sentence patterns, rather than by their referential meaning. Empty words are grouped according to the functions they signal: noun markers, verb markers, markers of prepositional phrases, clause markers, sentence connectors. Full words give clues to sentence patterns through their functional positions in sentence order; since empty words have little meaning except their structural functions, they provide invaluable clues to overall patterns and to smaller pattern parts. Reading instruction should take advantage of these important linguistic regularities that clarify the structure of sentence-level patterns that carry meaning.

Grammatical inflections are discussed in Chapter 7. Modern English is a relatively uninflected language, compared with modern Russian or German, or with its own Old English ancestor of a thousand years ago. Inflections, or word-form changes, are less important in our language than intonation, word order, and structure words. But the word-form changes we do have are important clues to structural patterns, and most of them are visually represented in writing and print—by regular spellings— as well as heard in speech. These changes of form are structural signals of grammatical and syntactical variations within the four great word classes of English: noun, verb, adjective, adverb— full words which carry specific meanings in addition to their class-identifying features.

Chapters 4 through 7 are central to this book. Word order, or function order in sentence patterns, is a most important clue to structure in American English sentences; since order can be clearly seen in print, and corresponds to speech intonation patterns, it should be stressed from the beginning in reading instruction. While we may illustrate sentence order with simple sentences using single words in the basic functions, as in *John loves Mary,* reading at any level of sophistication will require recognition of noun groups and verb groups and of noun and verb clusters in these functions; these groups and clusters may include not only adjectives and adverbs, but prepositional phrases and subordinate clauses; and clauses may be connected in ways other than by modification in the usual sense. American English sentences should be read—and children should be taught to read them— as series or sequences of structural functions signaled and patterned by intonation, by order of syntactical functions, by structure words, and to a lesser extent, by word-form changes. This would be truly reading by structures; it should yield maximum comprehension of meaning.

Twentieth-century language scholarship has also produced accurate information about spelling-sound relationships (phonics) and about the structure of American English words. These matters are taken up in some detail in Chapter 8. Though it may be assumed that the pupil will learn to analyze words sufficiently for his purpose by a guided inductive process as he learns to read, the reading teacher nevertheless must have linguistically sound knowledge of word structure and spelling, for whatever uses may be relevant to teaching the child to read, write, and spell. This knowledge should include an introduction to phonemics (study of basic sound units), the rudiments of morphemics (study of basic meaning-bearing units), word bases and affixes, and stress-pitch patterns that are important in word structure and function. Furthermore, the difference between syllabication in speech and in printing should be understood; (in general, printer's syllabication is a purely visual invention that has little bearing on the sound of words).

Chapter 9, "The Import of Language and of Reading," concludes the presentation. It is intended to open out a broad-perspective view of language, suggesting both its antiquity and its central, continuing importance to all mankind. Reading, a principal access to human culture, is seen as perhaps the chief means of humanizing people.

All references indicated by raised numerals in the text are listed, chapter by chapter, in a section of Notes following Chapter 9.

CHAPTER TWO

The reading problem in America

reading, we are told, can be a golden key to open golden doors —a truism. But it is a truism tending to obscure the fact that reading is a magic key only for children lucky enough to find it. What of the nonreaders who never get the talisman in their hands? They become the outcasts, the pariahs of our verbal-affluent society. Serious reading disability inflicts psychological wounds, financial and vocational penalties, and the shame of social stigma.

The fact is that many, many college students and adults, high school graduates all, are quite deficient in "sentence sense," the essential key to meaning-bearing structures in both reading and writing. They may be good spellers, and may even have impressive vocabularies as tested by items featuring single words out of context, but little sense of meaningful language structures in written or printed form. Whatever comprehension they can build rests on a shaky foundation. Such persons do not comprehend at all well in silent reading, nor do they read aloud with the native American English intonations—speech melodies and rhythms— that delineate the shape and pattern of our sentences and thus communicate meaning.

Yet in casual, running speech, most youngsters are linguistically skillful; with their companions they can be quite expressive, often sparkling with wit and humor. (It is true, of course, that they tend to clam up when faced by English teachers, or in public speech; but these are not questions of basic linguistic skill.) Our young people generally have more than adequate speech skills *outside of school;* their main problem is that they have not learned to read and write with any degree of skill. Yet successful reading and writing are absolutely essential to successful school work, or to study of any kind, in or out of school. Inability to read simply means that learning in all subjects may be stunted and sometimes hopelessly crippled at the very root. The golden ultimate goals of reading cannot so much as be glimpsed by victims of such stunting or crippling.

Everybody knows that we are forced to attempt remedial reading instruction throughout elementary school, beginning in the first grade, and to continue it through high school and into college and university. Untold numbers of graduates of accredited high schools score below the tenth-grade reading level on national norms at the point of college entrance; they enter higher schools where they either fail after attempting remedial work (too little and too late), or remain to force academic standards ever lower. One large municipal college regularly assigns 40 per cent of its entering freshmen to remedial reading classes because test scores show that *most of them read at or below the tenth-grade norm, three years or more below the norm for college freshmen.* Hundreds of those admitted are dropped at the end of the first semester for poor scholarship.

Everyone also knows that many children in our schools become excellent readers, but we cannot truly say why some succeed, while so many others miserably and tragically fail. Learning to read is a developmental task of such terrible import that many a youngster would no doubt master it if he had no more than printed materials to practice on and a native speaker who could read to answer his questions. *But bright children too often become poor readers.* In short, there is no reliable correlation between intelligence and reading ability, nor in fact between any other measurable human trait and reading ability. Meanwhile, our schools turn out too many crippled readers for anyone to rest comfortably with present solutions.

In May, 1960, in a front-page feature article, *The New York Times* published some startling facts about the reading retardation of children at the point of leaving elementary school and entering the seventh grade in New York City. Mentioning as contributing factors a former policy of promoting virtually all pupils regardless of their achievement, and the enrollment of some pupils who did not speak English, Dr. Joseph O. Loretan, associate superintendent in charge of the junior high schools, said that the situation was "deeply serious." Although elementary school graduates are supposed to have at least fifth-grade reading ability (two years *below* grade level), the article stated: "the survey found that 19,208 children in the seventh grade—the first year of junior high—had less than this. This number included almost a third of all pupils in the grade."

Moreover, it went on, "48,703 pupils, or 28 per cent, were two and a half years or more behind grade level, and 13,459, or nearly 8 per cent, were four and a half years or more behind. *About 5,000 children, including some in the ninth grade, are at first and second-grade levels.*" (Italics added.) This is official information issued by the public schools of the City of New York. The reading tests were taken by 94 per cent of the junior high school enrollment—172,632 pupils.[1] There is no reason to think that these conditions are more alarming than those of many other school systems, large and small.

Numerous reading authorities in their professional publications have also testified to the seriousness of our reading problem. W. P. Percival, studying why pupils do not pass in primary grades, noted that the highest number of poor readers is found in the first grade, but that only a slightly smaller number is found in the second grade. He states that 99 per cent of the failures in the first grade are due to poor reading ability; 90 per cent in the second grade; and 70 per cent in the third grade.[2] At the end of the third grade (K-3), children have already been in school *four years.*

Bond and Clymer, cited in Bond and Tinker, used a reading-expectancy formula of their own in an investigation of the reading abilities of 379 randomly selected children in the fifth grade. These investigators estimated expected percentages of disabled readers according to various decile points in scores on tests designed to give intelligence quotients (IQs). Their estimates are IQ of 90 to 100, 20 per cent disabled; IQ of 100 to 130, 14 per cent disabled; IQ of 130 to 140, 7 per cent disabled; IQ of 140 to 160, none. They also cite an expected 16 per cent of pupils with IQs in the 80s and 5 per cent of those in the 70s to be disabled readers.[3] An inherent difficulty of all such comparisons is the fact that most "IQ" tests contain a high proportion of verbal and reading items; poor readers obviously cannot do well on such tests of their "intelligence." Another investigator, Blair, does not make specific estimates, but assumes that many elementary school pupils will not read at grade level.[4]

In junior and senior high school, it has been estimated that one-fourth or more pupils may be disabled readers. Kottmeyer reported that 2,169 out of 7,380 *eighth-grade graduates* in St. Louis read at or below the national norms established for the *sixth grade*.[5] Reviewing Kottmeyer's data and the results of Traxler's 1946 testing of high school students, Witty commented that many teachers consider reading retardation the greatest obstacle to effective high school instruction.[6] Later in the same work Witty estimates that 15 or 20 per cent of *high school freshmen* read below the norms for the *seventh grade*.[7]

Other studies have shown that in many secondary schools, up to one-third of the students are poor readers, and 15 per cent are seriously retarded. Furthermore, DeBoer, Kaulfers, and Miller estimate that *2 per cent of high school freshmen are below fourth-grade norms, 30 per cent below seventh-grade norms, and 48 per cent below eighth-grade norms*.[8] It seems obvious that disabled readers in such high proportions must have a negative effect on the entire educational program.

Let us now consider some individual reading cripples.

George L is a most interesting case. When George came to the attention of a college reading specialist, he was twenty-six years old, employed as a semiskilled workman on production in a small factory, was married to a nice young woman, and the father of three preschool children. A graduate of an eight-grade school in a large city, George was well spoken, well mannered, and well dressed in conservative style. Mr. and Mrs. L were buying a modest home and attended church fairly regularly in their community. They drove a four-year-old car. The neighbors in their block of small homes considered them good neighbors and good parents. The Ls and all their friends believed they were a solid, well-married young couple.

When Mrs. L telephoned the college one afternoon and asked to talk to someone who could advise her about a reading problem, she was referred to the reading consultant. She told him that the problem had to do with her husband. She was quite distraught, and found it hard to control herself and remain coherent through the telephone interview. She said that she was having severe difficulties with her husband because he had become extremely cross with the children, and especially so with the oldest child, who was about ready to enter kindergarten.

When she remonstrated with her husband, he became defensively unpleasant with her too. Lately he had taken to staying away from home a good deal. She was not sure where he went, because he had recently lost his job, and seemed to her to be drifting. Their home was breaking up.

The reading consultant wondered what all this had to do with him. What was George L's trouble? Every night the oldest child was asking his father to read him children's stories from his little books. Somehow this ordinary request threw George into tantrums. Coincidentally, about this time he had been suddenly dismissed from the steady job he had held long enough to make both husband and wife feel it was a secure base for their humble life.

When George came to the college for a consultation, the reading specialist learned that he had, incredibly, never learned to read. George could not even read simple nursery tales. He had been fired by an irate foreman after he had triggered a costly production-line mixup because he had not read definite and clear printed instructions that had been issued to him. His foreman had been incredulous at first, but the simple truth was that George not only had not read the instructions, he was unable to read them—or to read anything at all. George's tantrums with the children and his staying away from his home and his loving wife were his only means of responding to a set of conditions that he could not rationally control. The reading consultant was forced to give up every means of testing except the interview itself, where he could show simple printed material to George while they talked and he could point to words and sentences. George was unable to recognize or call more than four or five isolated words: he had zero reading ability.

For over ten years, ever since his graduation from the eighth grade, George had been cleverly acting out a false role in American urban life, "passing" as a man who could read. He was normally intelligent. He had applied his intelligence to the problem of survival as an illiterate in a world where basic literacy is taken for granted. He had aimed to please, and he had succeeded. He had enjoyed a long series of pleasant everyday successes that came to him because of his good looks, good grooming, good manners, good conversation—and unfailing cooperativeness in all situations. He had made a profession of being a good boy. Above all, he had learned to profit from intelligent listening. Then all at once his false little world fell apart.

Since the college George had fled to as a desperate last resort offered no program for adults who read below the fifth-grade level, all the reading consultant could do was to refer him to a downtown agency that tried to teach immigrants a little speech, reading, and writing. But really no program could save George, nothing put Humpty Dumpty back together again. So far as the consultant ever knew, George disappeared into the city whence he came, and never was seen again except in an occasional haunting dream. How on earth could a thing like this have happened?

Most reading cripples who come to us in college are not so unusual as George, nor are their life crises so dramatic. The little we learn of some of them is merely suggestive.

A lovely young secretary in business, for example, well groomed and beautifully spoken, came to college part time to study "English" because of some difficulty about her job. A high school graduate, this pretty creature tested at the seventh-grade level in reading (more than five years below her level). She somehow passed the first semester of English composition but would surely have failed the second had she taken it; she barely managed to do low-average work in a noncredit remedial reading course. Completely unable to do college work, she dropped out without earning a single credit applicable to a degree, and without improving her secretarial skills. Who is she? What is she now? How many others are there like her?

Let us review briefly a few examples of the countless college freshmen whose weakness in reading is too great for them to overcome, even after two or three semesters of remedial instruction. In time, these young people either drop out of college voluntarily or are excluded for poor scholarship. No stereotype fits them. Many of them come from good middle-class homes in good neighborhoods, and have graduated from secondary schools of good reputation; they are not clinical cases, nor behavior problems in any sense. Many others come from poor homes in slum neighborhoods, associated with depressed ethnic groups.

Reading disability is no respecter of person, race, color, creed, or previous condition of servitude.

Let me cite two students who seem to exemplify extreme outcomes of the spelling-vocabulary approach to reading. Miss G excelled in the single-word memorization but was weak in comprehension; Mr. S achieved some comprehension despite his inability to focus on single words. It appears likely that both these students reflect (probably unconsciously) methods of reading instruction that exaggerate analysis and sounding of separate words outside the normal language structures in which they occur. Miss G may have been an over-cooperator, Mr. S a compulsive resistor. Let us look at them more closely.

Miss G was an attractive, well-groomed, pleasantly sophisticated girl, apparently from a cultivated Jewish home. Her reading comprehension tested just barely at the eighth-grade norm, her vocabulary barely at the ninth. Like many other reading cripples, she had been oversold on the importance of vocabulary—isolated words—and so in remedial reading she continued to memorize single words. She raised her knowledge of vocabulary items to the eleventh-grade level, but failed to improve her comprehension significantly. On scholastic probation at the beginning of her second semester in college, she was dropped at the end of it for poor scholarship.

Mr. S had a terrible psychological block on words—word identification and spelling—yet achieved a degree of comprehension in spite of this. His initial tests in reading placed him in the fifth grade in vocabulary and the sixth in comprehension. In remedial courses he showed considerable gains in comprehension and in his ability to summarize what he had read, but no improvement whatsoever in his ability to deal with individual words. He appeared to have such an unholy fear of words that he could not even look at a word and copy it correctly. His spelling would have caused a saint to weep. Yet he had no measurable difficulty attributable to poor visual acuity. How he might have fared under a different course of primary and elementary reading instruction, twelve years before he entered college, no one will ever know. Mr. S was a softly spoken, well-dressed, well-meaning, hard-working boy, quiet and cooperative, a graduate of a respectable high school in a good neighborhood. He was excluded for poor scholarship at the end of only two semesters of the easiest program offered by his college.

Mr. H typifies a large number of underprivileged Negro students who live in Negro tenement districts and attend large but academically poor high schools. A pleasant, likable lad, who at eighteen years seemed to have had about a sixth-grade education, Mr. H had to be closely supervised in the use of textbooks and workbooks. *He had to be taught how to use them.* At the beginning of remedial reading, his vocabulary tested at the seventh-grade level, his comprehension at the ninth; at the end of two semesters he had raised these scores to ninth and tenth, respectively. Dropped for poor scholarship.

Then there are the bright overprivileged students like Mr. C who, despite mediocre reading skills, do passable work, occasionally very good work, even in stiff science and math courses. His reading ability was at ninth-grade level when he entered, and rose to middle tenth after three remedial English and reading courses. He was then able to earn B grades in biology, mathematics, physical science, slide rule, humanities, and economic history. This boy completed college with some credit to himself, but he might have made Phi Beta Kappa if his reading ability had been at the level of his intellectual ability as demonstrated in a number of difficult courses.

Mr. R also exemplifies the freshman student of good intelligence from a fashionable neighborhood with exceptional schools; he finally obtained a college degree after partially repairing the damage of a very low level of reading skill at entrance: *sixth* grade. He took two remedial reading courses in sequence, studied diligently, requested and received extra instruction, and reached the tenth-grade reading level. This boy had unusual intelligence and critical ability, understood his problems, and cheerfully took advantage of his opportunity to solve them. He made a creditable college record, but like Mr. C, he did not perform very close to the level of his probable ability.

Can we learn anything from our crippled readers that may help us teach reading in such a way as to reduce their numbers in generations yet to come? What specific faults do they have that we might attempt to anticipate and thus perhaps prevent?

Above zero reading ability, typified by George L, the crippled reader's worst fault is literal word calling, or word-by-word reading, with virtually no sentence sense. *Reading cripples miss patterns of meaning because they miss the meaning-bearing patterns of language.* If they do not literally read word by word, they often read by arbitrary word groups or sentence fragments that make almost as little sense as isolated words called out one at a time. A somewhat more advanced common error is to read an introductory clause as if it were a complete sentence; or to "read" other sentence elements as if they were complete and independent structures. *All these structural errors cause failures in comprehension, since meaning cannot be reached except through the structures that carry meaning.*

Lacking a sure grasp of the printed sentence as the common building block of the paragraph and of the more extended forms of written discourse, the crippled reader cannot comprehend what he "reads" as organized, coherent form. Instead, he tends to register only arbitrary, random elements, and even to miss important language structures altogether in the material the writer sets before him. He sees a subject without its verb, a verb without its subject; he combines subjects with the wrong verbs and verbs with the wrong subjects; he attaches expanding phrases to the wrong sentence elements, or "reads" them by themselves, without any structural context. In this process he may retain a large number of isolated words, particularly if his basic reading instruction stressed memorizing single words: he will do better on the vocabulary than on comprehension of a test passage.

Greater attention should be given to developing sentence sense in reading and writing and less to learning individual words. It is probable that given a mastery of basic sentence structure, vocabulary would largely take care of itself, because basic sentence patterns of American English can be filled with an almost unlimited number of words. But no number of individual words can of themselves combine into a single structural and meaning-bearing language pattern. The remainder of this book concentrates on an explanation and display of our common language structures and relates them to basic reading and writing instruction.

CHAPTER THREE

*The child's language
from cradle
to kindergarten*

a language is a system—a learned arbitrary system of vocal symbols—functioning in a specific culture. A culture may be national, but within a nation—the United States, for example—many class, occupational, regional, and local subcultures exist. Each of these cultures possesses its own dialect with its own distinctive features; often the boundaries between such cultures and their dialects, though real, are vague and indistinct. Despite some barriers, and because of social mobility in American society, individuals cross these boundaries. Perhaps an *ultimate* aim of the public school program of native language instruction should be to develop freedom and fluency in the dialects used by persons carrying on the chief business of American society. But one of the *immediate* aims of the schools should certainly be to teach five- to seven-year-old children to read and write whatever dialect they were born to. This variant of the mother tongue can serve as a basis for language growth and development as nothing else can.

In this chapter I shall try to show why this is true. Precise information on the development of speech in infancy and early childhood, comparable in rigor to existing data on adult speech, is not yet available. The subject requires further research. What follows here is an interpretation of known data in the light of linguistic principles and of the author's own observations.

The child is born into a culture and a language. By the time he goes to school—between the ages of five and seven years—every normal child has mastered the basic structure system of his language, as well as the features of his class or regional dialect. And while these special dialectal features are superficial to American English—most Americans can understand each other's speech—they are obligatory upon the person born to any given dialect. The child hears this language and speaks it as a whole system, a closely interwoven fabric, not as a mosaic of tiny separate pieces. Where this speech differs from other speech, it differs systematically. Each child learns his native tongue by a tutelage of parents, brothers and sisters, playmates and teachers, mingling encouragement and punishment; this learning process is quite advanced when he first goes to school, and it continues in and out of school throughout his life.

Very shortly after he makes his difficult entry into this world, every healthy baby lets out a primordial squall, compounded of all the grief and discomfort, surprise, dismay, and indignation that he feels in his first moments of life. If he does not bawl as he is supposed to, his first disciplinary contact with life is administered by doctor or midwife—a sharp smack on the bottom while he is held upside down by the ankles. Then he gives forth the yawp that marks the beginning of breathing, life, and language. Very soon he learns to suck and swallow, to belch, drool, and burp, to murmur, whimper, and cry. This is the basis of his speech and his life; they are linked together. The beginning of his social life with man is the beginning of language for the baby.

Of the languages investigated, the baby "word" for *mother* is almost the same the world over: *ma-ma* in English, French, Italian, and Spanish, in Russian, Danish, Norwegian, Swedish, and Chinese. Physiology largely accounts for this; it might also be *ba-ba* or even *da-da.* In all languages, however, characteristic phonemic and intonational patterns are soon imposed upon the natural basic sounds, producing a native childhood term for *mother* in each culture.

Not only human babies, but calves, lambs, kids, pups, and kittens produce sounds resembling simple vowel phonemes simply by vocalizing and opening their mouths. If they vocalize before opening the lips, they produce the consonant sounds we mark /m/ and /b/ before the vowel sound. Even calves and lambs "say" something like *maa* if a relatively large amount of air passes through the nose, and *baa* if more air passes through the mouth. More precisely, *b* is a "stop" or momentary sound, produced at the moment the lips part. The *m* is a "continuant" that begins an appreciable length of time before the mouth or lips open. But to /ma/ and /ba/ is about as far as animal babies go in their development of "phonemes"; human babies with human tongues very soon can also say *da.* Since babies have no teeth, the tongue fits naturally against the toothless ridge; the stream of air carrying vocal sound through the open throat produces the consonant sound we mark /d/, at the instant the tongue is lowered to release the air: *Da!* Also, the various newborn baby sounds we spell *aw, waw, ow, wow* indicate the baby's early physiological production of some of the vowels and semivowels of the language he is already working on in his first hours and days of life.

At this uncontrolled stage of his linguistic development, the baby makes many of the sounds of American English, and sounds also that we as adults have forgotten how to make because they are not a part of our language system. He can make almost any "speech" sound, but *without linguistic consciousness or control.* He makes these sounds because he is a human being and because it is fun for him, though already his "speech" may be associated with his communication with other people. He makes Scottish, Irish, and Spanish burred "r" sounds, German gutturals, the uvular flick often called the Parisian "r," South African clicks, interdental (intergum) consonants not used in American English, vowel sounds, glides, liquids, semivowels, umlauts, and so on. He may produce them in an almost endless stream, with virtually unlimited repetition, and largely for his own amusement. This native spirit of playful experimentation should be nurtured in language instruction by parents and teachers at all levels of the learner's growth.

As the baby develops his first teeth, a larger and stronger jaw, and the complex chewing and masticating processes they contribute to, the specificity of his tongue movements increases until he is capable at the age of three or four of coming close to making almost any speech sound he wants to make. At the same time, through imitation, he has been sorting his sounds out and separating them into the distinctive speech sounds, or **phonemes,** of his native language. The ones he does not need he forgets and buries below conscious memory.

More important than the creation of the phonemic repertory, important as that is, is the development in early infancy of speech melodies and rhythms. These are the basis of the larger language patterns that he will master in a few years and carry through childhood, adolescence, and adult life. Cooing, murmuring, lallation, singing, crowing, laughing, crying, whimpering, swallowing with satisfaction (oral acceptance), vomiting and regurgitation with disgust (oral rejection)—all these activities, in association with the baby's life experiences, *especially in association with other people,* lay the foundation for the intonation patterns of his language.

American English has patterns of intonation that differentiate the larger utterances—statements, questions, requests; it also has subpatterns of intonation that delineate lesser elements within larger structures. The main features of intonation at the sentence level are pitch, stress, and juncture; pitch and stress patterns also differentiate lesser syntactical features. *These basic intonation patterns are obligatory, systematic throughout American English, and emotionally neutral.* They are not essentially self-expressive.

In studying the language as an arbitrary code of vocal symbols, many linguists distinguish strictly *linguistic* patterns from *paralinguistic* and *kinesic* features. The term *metalinguistics,* comprising both paralanguage and kinesics, is used by some linguists. *Kinesics* refers to gestures, facial expressions, shrugs, winks, and all such nonlingual and nonvocal communicative actions. *Paralanguage* means the expressive vocal distortions that accompany, or may accompany, the obligatory intonational patterning of language. We have all heard people laugh or cry as they talked, with more or less warping of the basic patterns. We are also familiar with the tones of acceptance or rejection in an utterance. These patterns and others like them are laid down in infancy and early childhood.

These interpretive aspects of speech that people use in communication with one another constitute an "overlay" of nonlinguistic features on the strictly linguistic patterns. This overlay is to some extent a learned patterning, integrated, however, with the developing personality (and dialect) of the child: he may apply it no more than half-consciously in his conversations. Professional actors and pantomimists raise paralanguage and kinesics to fine, sharply conscious performing arts, but the rest of us are adept at using these elements of language only half-consciously. The American English intonation system is treated in detail in Chapter 4, and then referred to and enlarged upon throughout the remainder of the book.

The baby's early experimental play with speech sounds begins with the physiological production of vowel and consonant phonemes and the tunes we popularly call cooing and crowing. Much of this early practice is more or less deliberate but involves only minimal linguistic consciousness: the sounds and movements practiced are not yet language, because they lack linguistic purpose and have little systematic meaning. But they are important as the base of all later development. Infants play imitatively with the stress, pitch, and juncture patterns of the speech they hear about them, varying the prattling game of intonations with the babbling game of phonemes.

There is no standard or "normal" age where *linguistic awareness* of these developments begins; the child may begin to work consciously on the language system as early as eight months of age, or as late as eighteen months. Large patterns of intonation usually develop before the child begins *consciously* to develop the basic sound units, the phonemes. It is almost uncanny to hear a child apparently talk, employing genuine native intonations for statements and questions, but entirely without specificity of sounds, words, or word groups; there is no "meaning," no statement, only the melodic and rhythmic contour suggesting utterances. Later, after he has acquired most of the phonemes, and some words, he will fill these general configurations of sound with specific meaning-bearing elements.

In this process there are swings from larger to smaller structural features as the child's interest shifts; no two children will proceed in exactly the same way. Teachers who are striving to develop the native language abilities of children can be confident that the larger structural patterns are primary in time, and basic. Native language learning is generally analytic rather than synthetic in its method: the speaker develops linguistic control by working in from larger structural patterns to smaller. Kindergarten-primary language arts and reading instruction should build upon this foundation. So should all language teaching.

The child's internal invention of his own version of the language is sufficiently complex, yet environment contributes further complexities that the teacher should thoughtfully note. Mama, daddy, grandma, grandpa, Aunt Tilly, and all the relatives may refrain from baby talk with the child. Good. Even so, they may adopt special modes of expressive intonation with the baby— quiet, restful, soothing, quiescent, unlike those of everyday talk with each other. His brothers and sisters at first, and later the children he plays with, will add their distinctive melodies and rhythms, and many adults will present different modes of intona- tion at various stages of his growth. At play, and in and out of school, he will also make linguistic-cultural contacts with other class and ethnic dialects, and with the inclusive-exclusive private languages created by children in groups to preserve their privacy and their individuality from adults and other enemies.

The child's world of language is rich and various in all linguistic elements; it develops from no simple mimicry of his parents' talk. It is worse than idle—it can be downright harmful —to attempt "corrections" of the child's developing speech when he is merely passing through phases of imitation and creation. He should be allowed to work it out himself, without purification from above. In his own time the child will discover and make his own the language and way of life suitable for him—if we do not interfere in unwitting, harmful ways. The adult attempting to influence the child's developing language intelligently, hu- manely, and on sound linguistic principles, will see himself as a model rather than as a policeman of language.

I have already spoken of the infant's natural physiological production of his speech sounds, and of his later process of sorting them into linguistically significant classes and contrastive pairs. These basic language units, the phonemes, are something like linguistic atoms. They combine into larger language units, the morphemes, that, similarly, are comparable to linguistic molecules. Most simple words are morphemes, as are prefixes and suffixes. The *l* and *k* sounds in *leak, like, luck,* and *look* are instances of two consonant phonemes, formed in slightly different parts of the mouth. The four vowel sounds stand in clear contrast to each other: in *leak* and *like* we have two different complex vowel nuclei, or so-called "long" vowels, $/ iy /$ and $/ ay /$, com- posed of two phonemes; in *luck* and *look* we have two simple vowel phonemes, or so-called "short" vowels, $/ ə /$ and $/ u /$.

The muscular action of tongue and mouth in forming the two

consonant sounds, / l / and / k /, differs slightly because of association with the related action of forming the nearby vowel sounds in the flowing stream of speech, which is continuous, not segmented. Thus, each consonant phoneme is modified somewhat by the vowel phoneme coming before (/ k /) or after (/ l /) because the articulatory movement that produces the consonant sound begins or ends differently. In the *leak, like, luck, look* series, there is a systematic, gradual shift of the point at which the word is articulated, from near the teeth in *leak* to well back in *look.* Saying the four words in sequence will demonstrate this shift. These differing positions are required by the different vowel sounds.

Each instance of the consonants / l / and / k / in these four words is an "allophone" of the phoneme; by definition, an allophone is a member of its phoneme class. *The phoneme is thus not a single sound, but a significant class of similar speech sounds.* Thus, the phoneme concept is an abstraction for a group of sounds distributed throughout the language. We do not notice differences between allophones, because we do not make any use of them in our language system: they are not linguistically significant. In other words, the / l / in *leak* is not significantly different from the / l / in *like, luck,* or *look;* they are all the same phoneme. But these "allophonic" (or phonetic) variations may give trouble to a foreign child who distinguishes different kinds of *l* sounds in his native language, that is, treats each different kind as a phoneme.

As noted earlier in this discussion, the baby physiologically produces a vowel sound with his mouth open and a consonant phoneme either with his mouth closed (a continuant), or as he opens or closes it (a stop). If his mouth is closed while he vocalizes, he makes the continuant *m;* if he opens it while he vocalizes, he emits a *b.* When he opens his mouth and exhales, he is reversing the process of eating, where he opens his mouth, sucks, and ingests the food; in vocalizing, he also vibrates the vocal folds, while in swallowing he closes them and holds them closed to keep food out of the larynx and windpipe.[1] His infant "speech," then, reversing the process of eating, constitutes a basic linguistic operation. Very early in life, and quite *unconsciously,* the baby begins to develop his system of vowel and consonant sounds: *ma, ba, pa, da, ta.*

The baby develops his phonemes by pairing them, on the principle of contrast. As already noted, *m* is a continuant and *b* is a stop, both using the same position of lips and teeth, and both involving vibrations of the vocal folds. The contrast is between stop and continuant. The *p* sound is like *b* except for vocalization, or voicing; the *p* sound is "unvoiced," or "voiceless." The contrast is between voice and no voice, but probably the baby is not conscious of the difference. His vowel sound in *ma* and *ba* is a back of the mouth sound, and may be contrasted with the vowel in *me, be,* or any "fronter" vowel sound. The pairing, or contrast, is between relative front and relative back mouth placement. In this way the newborn babe begins to construct his personal version of whatever dialect he was born into. A human baby is a human baby. Someday he will walk and talk like a man.

Just so each child builds his language. On the principle of contrast, by pairing sounds, his two consonants become three, then four, five, and six, eventually about twenty-one all told in American English. He contrasts his vowel phonemes by saying one with his lips wide open and another with his lips rounded, one up in the front of his mouth near the teeth and one high up at the back of the roof of his mouth, and so on, until he has eight or nine "simple" vowel phonemes ("short" vowels) and a number of diphthongs or complex vowel nuclei ("long" vowels). Using this sound system, he imitates the words and phrases he hears, combining phonemes into words and words into phrases within the intonation patterns he has practiced before, and imitating the various intonation patterns he hears now. He is not always very close to what is going to be his native tongue, and he even makes the old folks learn his language for a while. Like any other foreigner, he may say *zis, dis,* or *tis* for *this; witto* or *yiddo* for *little, wun* for *run* (the liquid sounds, *r* and *l,* are difficult for many children); *eben* for *even, firsty* for *thirsty,* and so on. In time most of these problems disappear. When adults finally say, "He talks nicely now," they are simply recognizing that he has adjusted his invented language system to theirs. A simple explanation of the physiological production of American English speech sounds, illustrated, may be studied in Appendix B, "The Human Speech Instrument," p. 216.

As we have seen, the child's invention of his language begins with large melodic and rhythmic patterns; it proceeds by wavelike movements from intonation to phonemes, phonemes to intonation, back and forth, up and down, all at once, an atom at a time, with large intervals at one time, short intervals at another. No two children begin at the same time nor proceed at the same rate. True *linguistic consciousness and control* develop unevenly in individual children, and there are great variations among different children. By the time a child goes to school, however, he has learned all the basic sentence patterns, their obligatory intonation patterns and word order, a good deal of functional grammar, including the system of word-form changes, and a vocabulary of more than five thousand words, including many of the three hundred or so structure words, such as *the, of, very, and, but, so.* Many children, especially those of educated parents who talk and read easily and freely, can substitute quite creatively within the basic sentence patterns and can spontaneously utter complex structures.

Following are samples of the free language of the four-year-old son of a college student:

This car is painted the same color as that submarine on TV.

I know it's not a good time to have candy now, but I was wondering if I can have some for "lunch dessert"?

(Explanation of a drawing): **This hippopotamus has a sharp thing on his back to use if other hippopotamuses aren't nice to him. He can't go in any hole. He's too big.**

It's good I sleep in the afternoon, because I don't get much sleep in the night.

(After being told about his mother's wedding): **When they played "Here Comes the Bride," and you were walking around, what was your name?**

You know, when I was a little baby I would say to myself, "Toe trucks carry toes." But they don't, do they?

Obviously a bright little fellow, with excellent command of language at the age of four, his chief advantage was being born into a literate home, of adult and affectionate parents who accepted him and loved him.

Often children who have a good command of the language make logical mistakes involving irregularities they have not yet encountered in the system. One such intelligent error is using "regular" past or past participle forms for irregular verbs: *gived* for *gave*, *buyed* for *bought*, *teached* for *taught*, *runned* for *ran*, *do'ed* for *did*; or using "regular" noun plural forms for irregular nouns: *mans* for *men*, *childs* or *childrens* for *children*, *womans* for *women*, *mouses* for *mice*, *deers* for *deer*, *moneys* for *money* (often meaning the plural *coins*). All these misconstructions prove that the children using them are accurately aware of the *regular* structural forms for two important word classes, verbs and nouns. How can they be expected to know the irregularities and inconsistencies so soon?

A word on reading readiness. Probably the best way to prepare a very young child for reading is to hold him in your lap and read aloud to him, over and over again, stories that he likes from the world's treasury of children's literature, *while the child follows the text with eyes and ears*. Thus, with the printed page before him, the learner enjoys a real introduction to the relationship of graphic symbols to language. The printed page talks. It talks on purpose to the child. The cozy comfort and protection of the adult's lap, the exclusive attention, the general euphoria of the relaxed, kindly, dramatic tone of voice for reading aloud to a young child, the make-believe and faraway world of the book itself, walling in reader and child, and walling out the rest of the world—basking and bathing in this sea of dreams is a near-perfect initiation into reading and the world of books. Many children learn to read sentences with their eyes and to associate the spoken patterns and melodies so well that they will protest any omission of word or phrase in a familiar story they are avidly following—sentence by sentence and page by page. Some adult readers check the child's attentiveness or playfully tease him by deliberate omissions, changes, and additions, making a game of it all. Many children have learned to read in this exciting, painless way before going to school and studying phonics, letters, isolated words, and before reading repetitive stories designed to teach a controlled vocabulary.

Teachers and parents have been in despair for years over the fractured English and idiotic story line built into the controlled-vocabulary "attack" on primary reading. These materials have become a chronic national pain; so much so that a writer in a national magazine for adults could successfully communicate his satirical message by writing in the unconscionable "style" of so-called basal readers.

LOOK! LOOK! SOMEONE IS IN THE GARDEN

Look.
Look. See. Look and see the house. The house is white. It is a white house.
The white house has a garden.
What is in the garden?
There is grass in the garden. The grass is green.
There is something else in the garden.
What is it?
It is a football.
Is the football lost? Who lost the football? Did Jack lose the football?
Yes. See Jack looking for the football. Jack is in the garden by the white house looking for the football.
It is a touch football.
Wait!

Jack sees the football. Jack does not pick up the football. Is Jack looking for the football? No! Jack is looking for something else. What is Jack looking for?
Look.
See Bobby. Here comes Bobby.
See Bobby in the garden with Jack. Jack and Bobby are in the garden.
What are Bobby and Jack doing in the garden?
They are looking for the football.
No. They are not looking for the football. Jack and Bobby are looking for something else.
Wait!
Here comes father.
What is father doing in the garden?
Father, Bobby and Jack are looking in the garden. . . .[2]

Successful communication in this instance depends entirely upon the fact that American adults are familiar *ad nauseam* with the similar style and content of reading textbooks for children.

In connection with reading readiness, it is interesting that some preschool children undoubtedly learn to read by their own spelling method. Not so lucky as children who have listened to enchanting books read aloud to them by fond adults, such children nevertheless somehow learn for themselves that *words are graphic representations of things they can say and hear.* They study the labels on boxes of soap or breakfast cereal, signs along the street, billboards, newspaper and magazine titles, television captions and advertising, anything, everything in print. They ask to hear what words these graphic symbols say. They ask how to spell the words. What are the letters, from left to right? How do you say the names of the letters? They say the words and the names of the letters aloud. They copy them. It is not much of a step for these children to ask how to reverse the process and write what they say. At this point they do not need to be able to "sing" the alphabet as an arbitrary sequence of letters: they do know the alphabetical principle through knowing the names of many letters and some of the sounds the letters may represent.

CHAPTER FOUR

Intonation:
the melodies
of the printed page

Simply by talking, the child who goes to school demonstrates his mastery of the basic structures of American English. His speech reflects the language of family and playmates, though he may still carry traces of baby talk. With little intervention of teacher and school, life itself may eliminate nonfunctional or inappropriate characteristics of immature speech or "undesirable" dialect features; but life may also perpetuate them, regardless of well-intentioned efforts to change them. Changing a child's dialect, as distinct from clarifying his use of language, cannot be achieved merely by a teacher (or a curriculum); it is a complex psychosociological process involving teachers, family, and childhood friends, but above all, his own goals and aspirations—the image the child develops of himself.

A child's language is an intensely personal possession; it has already cost him years of struggle, a little heartbreak, and probably an occasional bloody nose as he explored the ways of children and men. He will change and develop his language throughout life to correspond to changing circumstances, immediate needs, ultimate ambitions. But this is not to deny the crucial role of the school in making him literate. Quite the contrary: teachers and parents need to deepen their linguistic understanding and thus clarify the role of formal schooling in the child's growing command of his language. Language is a powerful social bond, integral with both personality and culture; given sufficient insight and intelligence, the school may strengthen the child's grasp of language so as to free him from unnecessary restraints and enable him to function in socially useful and personally satisfying ways.

Since the child entering school is already experienced at an unconscious level in the basic signals and structures of his language, primary reading and writing instruction should begin with developing his consciousness of them in relation to the graphic system. Probably the best method is *practice in speaking and oral reading of familiar patterns, with emphasis upon the native intonations.* If we really want him to learn reading and writing —to become literate—we should not attempt instead to convert him to another dialect, nor to "purify" his speech. We should teach him the relationship of entire sentence patterns—in his own speech—to their graphic counterparts; that is to say, to language structures as represented in the systems of writing and print. This is the essence of reading American English *as a native language process;* its ultimate development may take the better part of a lifetime.

Underlying our language structures is intonation, yet our awareness of its importance is very recent. Most linguists agree that intonation is the structural feature that particularly distinguishes native accent from foreign. So far, the application of intonation data to the teaching of American English has been pretty well limited to punctuation, but it may turn out to be decisive in teaching American children to *read* their own language—as well as to *write* it—more easily and efficiently.

To improve his preparation for teaching reading, an attentive native speaker of American English, with the help of a book like this one, can make sufficiently detailed observations of the tunes and rhythms of his own speech and the language of the people around him. A tape recorder is invaluable in making such observations. A native speaker can also develop ability to read aloud, deliberately but naturally, so as to learn for himself how the graphic counterparts of the language system provide useful clues to the melodies of the printed page. It is not necessary to cultivate technical linguistic competence in making fine distinctions of relative pitch, stress, and juncture (the separate elements of intonation). What is necessary is adequate variety and specificity of observation to make the native speaker conscious of the principal intonation patterns of his language. Such consciousness should be applied in teaching the child how to read his own language as he naturally speaks it, trippingly on the tongue.

In oral reading—the basis of the child's later development of silent reading—normally only one word in each sentence should receive a maximum or "heavy" stress (accent). This is a general rule of speech that should be followed in reading aloud. Word-by-word reading, or reading by pattern fragments, is characterized by several heavy stresses in each sentence; in literal word-by word reading, a common disability, each word takes a heavy stress, along with a simultaneous falling pitch and voice fadeout. But this is the intonation that indicates completion or finality in American English: normally, a medium or heavy stress occurs only on the last word of a structural element, or on the word that concludes an utterance. This heavy stress is often accompanied by a falling pitch contour that ends with what I shall call a "fade-fall terminal" of the stream of speech.

Within the sentence are patterns of stress and pitch that are readily accessible and familiar to us all. For example, in English there is a large class of paired two-syllable words, generally of classic origin, one a noun and the other a verb; relative stress placement and the accompanying voice pitch differentiate them. Most of us are aware of the stress differences; perhaps not all have noted the change of pitch. In such a pair as *cónflict* and *conflíct*, a heavy stress on the first syllable, followed by a weak stress and a *falling* pitch on the second, signals that the word is a noun; a heavy stress on the second syllable, *accompanied by a rising pitch*, signals that the word is a verb. In these pairs, the relative differentials of pitch and stress, which together form a pattern of intonation, are structural signals of the grammatical distinction between noun and verb. This *relative difference of stress within the word* maintains itself regardless of the placement of heavy stresses in larger sentence elements containing the word.

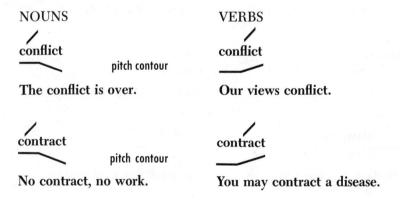

NOUNS

conflict   pitch contour

The conflict is over.

contract   pitch contour

No contract, no work.

VERBS

conflict

Our views conflict.

contract

You may contract a disease.

NOUNS	VERBS
⟋address ⎯⎯⟍ pitch contour	⟋address ⎯⎯⟋
Do you have my address?	Please address us here.
⟋rebel ⎯⟍ pitch contour	⟋rebel ⎯⟋
He was a rebel.	It does no good to rebel.
⟋import ⎯⎯⟍ pitch contour	⟋import ⎯⟋
It is a foreign import.	We will import it.

A similar pattern of intonation may be observed in word pairs in which a verb-adverb group has kept its first intrinsic structure and function, but by substitution in larger patterns has also developed a noun position and use. Examples include:

NOUNS	VERB-ADVERB GROUPS
⟋setup ⎯⟍ pitch contour	⟋set up ⎯⟋
I don't like the setup.	It was nicely set up.
⟋breakup ⎯⎯⟍ pitch contour	break ⟋up ⎯⎯⟋
The breakup came late.	The ice did not break up early.
⟋markdown ⎯⎯⟍ pitch contour	mark ⟋down ⎯⟋
There was a markdown of prices.	We mark down all items.

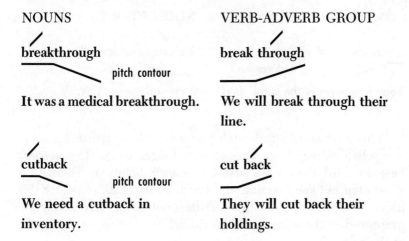

NOUNS	VERB-ADVERB GROUP

breakthrough
pitch contour

It was a medical breakthrough.

break through

We will break through their line.

cutback
pitch contour

We need a cutback in inventory.

cut back

They will cut back their holdings.

In silent reading, as well as in oral reading and speech, additional clues such as noun and verb markers may also help to differentiate the positions and uses of these pairs.

Similar contrasts of stress-pitch patterns distinguish compound words from the noun groups they derive from:

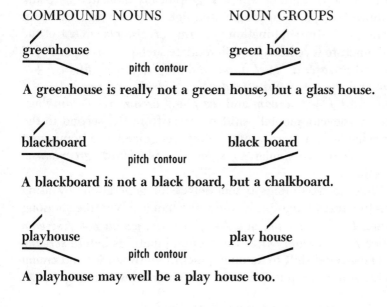

COMPOUND NOUNS	NOUN GROUPS

greenhouse
pitch contour

green house

A greenhouse is really not a green house, but a glass house.

blackboard
pitch contour

black board

A blackboard is not a black board, but a chalkboard.

playhouse
pitch contour

play house

A playhouse may well be a play house too.

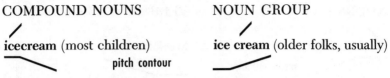

COMPOUND NOUNS	NOUN GROUP
⟋	⟋
icecream (most children)	**ice cream** (older folks, usually)
⟍ pitch contour	⟍

Your icecream is the same as my ice cream.

This contrast of stress-pitch patterns is the linguistic basis for a baseball riddle: Why does it take longer to go from second base to third than from first to second? Solution: There is a *short stop* between second and third. In baseball, of course the player is a *shortstop;* either of the contrasting terms may be presented as the solution of the riddle, depending on the whim of the riddler.

Another distinctive intonation contrast is often heard in the *icecream* and *ice cream* pair: a faint "cut" or separation between *ice* and *cream* occurs in the noun group but not in the compound word. This cut, which sets off one word or one syllable from the next, is an "open" juncture, indicated by a plus mark in linguistic notation / + /. The more carefully articulated speech is, the more frequently open juncture occurs. In oral reading, it often marks the separation of words as graphically indicated by blank or unprinted spaces in the printed line; it is also an element of certain pitch-stress intonation patterns. Precise placement of the open juncture is required to differentiate such pairs as *night / + / rate* and *nitrate; a / + / name* and *an / + / aim; flight / + / wrap* and *fly / + / trap; need a / + / drain* and *needed / + / rain;* and *I / + / scream* and *ice / + / cream. Ice cream* illustrates a "developmental" shift of stress from the second to the first syllable in a word group being recognized as a compound word—*icecream*—similar to *sidewalk, blackbird, greenhouse,* and others.

Children have amused themselves for generations by using open junctures humorously and interchangeably in the singsong refrain, *I / + / scream, you / + / scream, we all / + / scream for ice / + / cream.* After three open junctures before *scream,* the unexpected shift to an open juncture between *ice* and *cream* has the force of a punch line in a radio or television gag. Something similar is heard in the children's joke about the outcome when the songbird went through the lawn mower: **shredded tweet.** This is pure linguistic play; here, another sound / t / is added after the open juncture to produce a clever and nimble word play on **shredded wheat.** The old song of "Mairzy Doats" is another funny example of scrambled junctures and phonemes. Using elisions of words in place of open junctures, **Mairzy doats and dozey doats and liddle lamzy divey** is a transmogrification of **Mares eat oats and does eat oats and little lambs eat ivy.**

Likewise the tongue-twisting, ear-teasing riddle: **What kind of a noise annoys an oyster?** And its tricky solution: **A noisy noise annoys an oyster.** The sharp linguistic humor involves a natural elision of words that nearly excludes word-separating junctures. Moreover, the two utterances have, within themselves and between the pair, identical, repetitive stress patterns and pitch contours. In both question and answer there is an amusing contrast of the sounds represented by the letter **s** in "annoys" / z / and in "an oyster" / s /. The sole contrast between the riddle and the solution is the addition of the word **noisy** with its final vowel contrasting in "noisy noise" ("long e") with the first vowel of **annoys** in "noise annoys" ("schwa sound"). These gross similarities and fine contrasts make for great hilarity in this engaging little nonsense.

Children crack up over such shenanigans with words and language. They relish their own linguistic sophistication, and delight in manipulating language skillfully in intricate patterns. Why not join the fun?

Open juncture is a sharp cut in the speech stream between words or between syllables. Another way of setting off words, word groups, or even whole utterances, is to terminate the sound at the end of the structure with a slight rise in pitch during which the voice trails off into silence. This speech "terminal," marked with a rising arrow / ➚ / in linguistic notation, is fairly reliably signaled within sentences in writing and print by the comma; though not obligatory, a rise in the pitch contour may precede and lead into this terminal. Perhaps the clearest, most readily accessible examples of this rise in the pitch contour ended by a fade-rise terminal may be heard in counting, or in any list or series. The fade-rise terminal marks the end of each item in a series except the last, where a different pattern marked by a fade-fall terminal is obligatory. When accurately placed, commas are limited but important visual clues to intonation patterns.

PRINTED: **One, two, three, four, five.** (Counting)

Pitch
contour ⌣   ⌣   ⌣   ⌣

SPOKEN: **One** / ⌒ / **two** / ⌒ / **three** / ⌒ / **four** / ⌒ /

five / ⌒ /

PRINTED: **Bread, jam, pears, ham, and eggs.** (List, or series)

Pitch
contour ⌣   ⌣   ⌣   ⌣

SPOKEN: **Bread** / ⌒ / **jam** / ⌒ / **pears** / ⌒ / **ham** / ⌒ /

and eggs / ⌒ /

Native speakers may vary their individual intonation patterns from any "norm." They may count rapidly, running the numbers together, they may separate the units of series with fade-rise or fade-fall terminals—and also with rising and falling pitch contours—depending on rate of speech and degree of emphasis. In any event they conclude with the obligatory fade-fall terminal, to signal the end of the utterance, often preceded by a falling pitch contour leading into the final terminal. Within the utterance, the fade-rise terminal indicates that the utterance is not complete but continues. The fade-fall terminal signals the conclusion of the utterance. Its significance is finality.

In basic reading instruction, children should be encouraged to read series orally, and also to count, nimbly and rhythmically, using the normal rising tones of speech. Children at play enjoy counting games and songs with musical tunes and rhythms that reflect their control of American speech melodies, as in hopscotch, skipping rope, or bouncing a ball. In the game of O'Leary, the child bounces a ball to the rhythm and tune of a lilting song. After every third bounce, he calls "O'Leary," and lifts and crosses one leg over the ball as he bounces it under and catches it on the other side. Children call this entire special movement an "O'Leary."

In the O'Leary song, the child's voice rises on the successive counts, generally rises on the three series of counts, and then on the last line of the stanza, very distinctly falling on the last word, signaling the end, when the graceful little game is over.

One, two, three, O'Leary, / ⟋ /
                  (Bounce, bounce, bounce, and over)

Four, five, six, O'Leary, / ⟋ /
                  (Bounce, bounce, bounce, and over)

Seven, eight, nine, O'Leary, / ⟋ /
                  (Bounce, bounce, bounce, and over)

Ten O'Leary, postman. / ⟍ /
                  (Bounce, and over, bounce, bounce)

If teachers and parents keep such rhythmic songs and games in mind, and teach oral reading of rising-tone patterns where they occur in speech, children will be less likely to read orally with more than one falling tone for each complete sentence. Oral reading with many falling tones and heavy stresses accustoms the child to reading by structural pattern fragments, even word by word. A child so taught is a potential reading cripple, unable to move freely and comprehendingly among the larger structural patterns that convey meaning. *Young learners learn what they practice.*

Language instruction aims for the development of "sentence

sense" in all language processes—auding, speaking, reading, writing. (*Auding* is defined in the Introduction, on page xx, item 14.) The fundamental means of distinguishing sentences from "nonsentences" is thorough familiarity with basic intonation patterns. American English intonation consists of relative pitch, relative stress, and related junctures and terminals; these combine into melodies and rhythms of statements, questions and requests or commands. It is primarily these intonation patterns that make our accent American.

These large rhythmic and melodic contours are characterized by final patterns that signal what the completed structure is. The final intonation pattern defines the whole. Primarily, English utterances are understood as sentences because they end with one of the end-signaling patterns, not because of their word order or the particular words within larger patterns. Native rhythms and melodies of American speech have been described by linguists in greater detail than is necessary for basic teaching of reading and writing. If teachers and parents know the bare structural essentials of our sentence tunes, they can teach effectively. But these bare essentials are really essential.

In reading and writing instruction, as clear a distinction as possible should be made between two basically different kinds of intonation signals: (1) *syntactical* patterns that are grossly but incompletely represented in the graphic system; and (2) *interpretive* "overlays," including numerous "vocal qualifiers" (in common parlance "tone of voice") that cannot be directly represented in the graphic system: they must be stated or described in the text. Syntactical and grammatical intonations are, in the narrow sense of the term, strictly *linguistic* features of American English; in contrast, the interpretive features of intonation are, broadly, *paralinguistic*.

Paralinguistic or interpretive intonations are optional; emotionally subjective, expressive of biases, attitudes, and immediate feeling, they vary according to personality, situation, and circumstances. They also vary by dialect. Native speakers use the obligatory intonation patterns naturally, and superimpose optional features naturally on these structural bases. Linguistic and paralinguistic features of intonation are often difficult to separate.

More research is needed to develop descriptions of interpretive and dialectal uses of the complex overlay of such vocal qualifiers as overhighness, overloudness, oversoftness, or muting; drawling or clipping; rasping, openness, or hollowness; breaking or whining; and singing or whispering; as well as systematic variations of pitch, stress, or juncture. In the meantime, however, we have useful approximate analyses.

Kinesics also is important to speech. Kinesics includes many nonlinguistic characteristics of communication, such as facial expressions and bodily movements—shrugs, nods, winks, gestures of all kinds, large and small. These physical and visible reinforcers of meaning are a fascinating and important topic, but since kinesics is not represented in the writing system, we merely mention it and pass on.

Both syntactical and interpretive intonations are important in American speech and in oral interpretation; but in *basic* reading and writing instruction, the syntactical are fundamental and the interpretive largely irrelevant. For this purpose, syntactical and interpretive intonations should be differentiated as sharply as possible, not blurred nor confused: the syntactical are characteristic of the language as code; the interpretive, ultimately, of the language as a basis for art. The first problem in reading and writing instruction is to develop the child's mastery of the graphic representation of his language as code, and a commensurate ability to move back and forth freely between the primary (audio-lingual) and the secondary (manual-visual) symbol systems of that code. Without a firm control of the code, the child can never develop an adequate appreciation of the artistic aspects of his language.

Suppose someone asks, "Where are the graphic symbols for intonation to be found upon the silent printed page?" *Everything in a written or printed sentence contributes to the graphic representation of the sentence as a whole.* Since every sentence has an underlying high-frequency syntactical intonation pattern, all that appears in the written or printed line helps to indicate that pattern. Taken all together, then, the graphic symbols visually delineate entire language patterns, sentences in particular, and thus remind the tongue and the ear of normal sentence tunes.

These inherent melodies and rhythms of native speech, these tunes, are what is meant by intonation patterns. Here we are considering only the underlying high-frequency syntactical features of intonation, not the interpretive vocal qualifiers that native speakers may overlay upon the basic patterns, at will.

Probably the most easily understood obligatory intonation feature in American English is the fade-fall terminal that signals the conclusion of three sentence-level utterances: declarative statements, commands or requests, and many questions. Frequently preceded by a falling pitch contour, this syntactical intonation feature of general American speech, used unconsciously by native speakers, is the most common concluding pattern. In linguistic notation it is marked by a falling arrow: / ⟶ /.

For reading instruction, it is particularly significant that this is the intonation pattern of any word when it is uttered singly, as, for example, in one-word answers to questions in everyday conversations.

Are you ready to go?	Yes. / ⟶ /
When will it come?	Tomorrow. / ⟶ /
Where have you been?	Playing. / ⟶ /
What else do you need?	Money. / ⟶ /
Where are you going?	Lunch. / ⟶ /

If school children study and practice reading single words in isolation or in structureless groupings, however, this natural pattern of one-word answers may become confused with unnatural patterns and unnatural intonations. Reading isolated words, or reading vertical or horizontal lists from the board or from books, is bound to produce the intonation pattern of finality on every single word. This practice will then contribute to that word calling in primary reading that leads to patternless "word perception" without comprehension of either structure or meaning.

In writing and print, this final terminal is graphically signaled by the whole sentence pattern and the final punctuation. Statements, requests, and many questions, when read aloud naturally and deliberately, in a neutral emotional tone, will usually produce the characteristics of a conclusive intonation; *on or after the word which receives a heavy stress, the pitch falls below the general level at which the pattern has been spoken; and the sound of the voice drops slightly as it fades away.* This slight dropping with simultaneous fading at the very end of the voice sound is the fade-fall terminal.

The technique of natural but somewhat stylized oral reading suggested here requires genuine linguistic consciousness, as well as ear training and practice; even when used skillfully, the evidence it yields is not of a rigor comparable with that of analysis of consonant and vowel phonemes, or morphemes, or of word order in phrase, clause, and sentence patterns. Oral reading to discover our native intonation patterns can be very useful, nevertheless, and deserves serious study and practice by all who handle American English language processes in their teaching.

American English intonation patterns involve four relative levels of pitch, which are designated, from lowest to highest— **low, normal, high, highest**—abbreviated **l, n, h, hh.** Level **n, normal,** is the pitch range most commonly used to initiate sentences; in calm, deliberate speech, only three levels are used in an utterance: levels **l, n,** and **h.** These pitch levels are *relative,* as between one speaker and another, and between utterances of the same speaker at different times, on different occasions, under different circumstances. They are also relative in the sense that they do not represent notes on the musical scale, but rather *a distinctive range* of speech tones that, taken all together, constitute *a linguistically significant pitch level.*

Pitch in speech also differs qualitatively from musical pitch in that a speech tone is never held in the way a song note is held; in fact, the moment a speech tone is held it loses its specific quality as a speech tone and becomes a song note. This is the difference between speech tones and song notes: the *musical* range of the speaking voice may be measured by just this device of holding a speech tone on pitch—singing it—and then locating it on a piano keyboard. The melodies of speech are a subtle and elusive music which requires as much ear training as singing for clear reception of the finer details. But the main syntactical features of intonation will yield to study.

The most common concluding intonation pattern is heard in speech and oral reading at the point marked with a falling arrow / ↘ / in the following simple examples. Preceding the fade-fall terminal, the pitch contour often falls one pitch level. Correspondingly, *this intonation should be picked up by the mental ear in reading the entire pattern and noting the final punctuation.*

STATEMENTS: identical final pattern

PRINTED: **John walked.**   **They came late.**

SPOKEN: John walked / ↘ /   They came late / ↘ /

PRINTED: **Everyone went to the party.**

SPOKEN: Everyone went to the party / ↘ /

PRINTED: **Bob rode.**

SPOKEN: Bob rode / ↘ /

QUESTIONS: signaled by initial question words—which, what, who, where, why

PRINTED: **Which one?**   **Who dealt this mess?**

                n——— ⬎⟍| pitch contour n——— ——— ——⟍
SPOKEN: **Which one** / ⟿ /   **Who dealt this mess** / ⟿ /

PRINTED: **Who said it?**   **Where's the car?**

                n——— ——— ⟍| pitch contour   n——— ——— ——⟍|
SPOKEN: **Who said it** / ⟿ /   **Where's the car** / ⟿ /

PRINTED: **Why worry?**

                n——— ⟍| pitch contour
SPOKEN: **Why worry** / ⟿ /

REQUESTS:

PRINTED: **Come over to tea.**

                n——— ——— — ⟍| pitch contour
SPOKEN: **Come over to tea** / ⟿ /

PRINTED: **Please have some cake.**

                n——— ——— ——— ⟍| pitch contour
SPOKEN: **Please have some cake** / ⟿ /

While in expressive speech and oral reading it is possible to utter these language patterns (and most others) with various paralinguistic overlays, or interpretive features, *the basic structural intonation* usually remains constant—especially the distinctive fade-fall terminal. This fact is invaluable in teaching sentence sense in both reading and writing.

There are some obligatory exceptions to the falling pitch contour preceding the fade-fall terminal that together frequently mark questions. One exception is the familiar device of converting a statement or request into a question solely by a rising pitch contour leading into a final fade-rise terminal. Another involves changing a simple straightforward question into a question of special intent by the same intonation device: for example, an implicit request for a repetition of the statement that motivated the question, or an expression of surprise, incredulity, regret, or the like.

Any of the examples above of statements or requests can be converted into questions by means of a rising pitch contour ended by a fade-rise terminal. Then the question mark would appear (rather late in the pattern) as a graphic indication of the intended final intonation feature, further indicated in the following examples by the rising arrow / ⟍ /.

CONVERTED STATEMENTS:

PRINTED: **John walked?**

                                                    pitch contour
SPOKEN: **John walked / ⟍ /**

PRINTED: **They came late?**

                                                    pitch contour
SPOKEN: **They came late / ⟍ /**

PRINTED: **Come over to tea?**

                                                    pitch contour
SPOKEN: **Come over to tea / ⟍ /**

PRINTED: **Please have some cake?**

                                                    pitch contour
SPOKEN: **Please have some cake / ⟍ /**

PRINTED: **Everyone went to the party?**

                                                    pitch contour
SPOKEN: **Everyone went to the party / ⟍ /**

Another and amusing use of the same intonation pattern to convert a statement into a question is often heard in such ironical remarks as these.

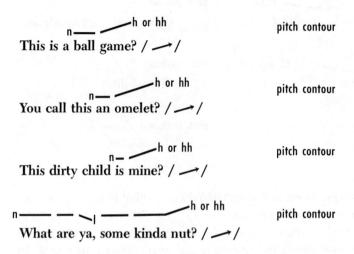

This is a ball game? / ⟋ /   pitch contour

You call this an omelet? / ⟋ /   pitch contour

This dirty child is mine? / ⟋ /   pitch contour

What are ya, some kinda nut? / ⟋ /   pitch contour

The fade-rise terminal is obligatory in these meanings; in print it is reliably signaled by the question mark, though late.

The other exceptional fade-rise terminal in a question pattern is common enough in speech, but since it is entirely optional with the speaker, we have no graphic device to represent it in writing or print. This intonation pattern often suggests a real incredulity, or just as often feigned disbelief; or it may signal a request for a repetition of a statement or an answer just given. Sometimes it identifies a question involving some form of special emphasis, verging on paralanguage.

When did it happen? / ⟋ /   pitch contour   (Request for repetition)

What did you say? / ⟋ /   pitch contour   (Request for repetition)

n_____ /‾h or hh   pitch contour
Has it finally happened? / ⟋ /   (Grief, regret, relief)

n_____ __ /‾h or hh   pitch contour
Weren't you ready? / ⟋ /   (Exasperation, impatience)

n___ /‾h or hh   pitch contour
Is this the boy? / ⟋ /   (Incredulity)

n⌣h or hh   pitch contour
What? / ⟋ /   (Incredulity, disbelief)

These questions and others like them (probably most questions, in fact) can be spoken or read aloud with either the *typical* fade-fall terminal or the *exceptional* fade-rise terminal, at the option of the person asking the question and according to his intent. In reading, the context will usually furnish clues to the writer's meaning, but the writer himself has no graphic symbol to indicate which intonation pattern he intends. In writing a question, he is obliged to use the question mark; only some additional explanatory or descriptive statement can signify special intent. Lacking such an explicit indication, the reader usually should assume the fade-fall terminal, because it is the normal, high-frequency, or obligatory characteristic of the intonation pattern signaling a question in American English. It is frequently preceded by a falling pitch contour.

Long questions are perhaps more frequently uttered with a final fade-fall terminal than short questions. The short-question inversions using the forms of *be* and *have,* and short questions using *will* and the forms of *do* as initial question markers, in particular, commonly end with a fade-rise terminal often preceded by a one-level rise in the pitch contour.

Am I? / ⟋ /   **Are you?** / ⟋ /   **Is he?** / ⟋ /

Have we? / ⟶ /   Have you? / ⟶ /   Has he? / ⟶ /

Do you know? / ⟶ /   Did he say? / ⟶ /

Does he agree? / ⟶ /

Will you play? / ⟶ /   Will she go? / ⟶ /

Will they accept? / ⟶ /

These are simple formulas of conversation and of dialogue, how-ever, rather than patterns of prose. They are more applicable to everyday speech—and to work with experience charts and writing simple plays—than to reading and writing above the primary level.

Countless students say that they were taught in school to use the question mark *only* where they hear a high-rising final pitch in speech, and to produce a high-rising pitch in oral reading *every time* they utter any kind of question. Moreover, students also say that they were taught to use a comma, a semicolon, or a period—but especially to use a comma—wherever they hear a "pause" in speech. They say they were taught that in oral reading they should "pause" wherever they see one of these punctuation marks, and nowhere else. This is inaccurate and misleading advice.

There are, in fact, numerous cuts or junctures in oral utter-ances, but only two are systematically represented by punctuation marks suggesting high-frequency or obligatory intonation features. They are the fade-rise and the fade-fall terminals illustrated above. So far, this discussion has demonstrated that the normal or obligatory characteristic of many questions is the same fade-fall terminal that marks most statements and requests; frequently, a one-level drop in pitch precedes this terminal. The remainder of this chapter introduces the other common features of American English intonation and relates them to their graphic counterparts in writing and print. Let us begin with a concise statement describing the basic system of junctures and terminals.

The stream of speech sound can be interrupted or terminated

in two ways: as the sound ends, it can be cut off sharply, or it can be allowed to trail off into silence. Pitch may be treated in three ways as a feature of these two terminations: (1) it may rise slightly or (2) it may fall slightly; otherwise (3) pitch is sustained or held "level." American English junctures are simple combinations of these three pitch treatments with the two ways of cutting off the stream of sound.

After the open juncture / + / and after the sustained, or level terminal / ⟶ /, the pitch is held steady and the sound is cut off more or less sharply; there may or may not be a distinct interval of silence after the cut, before the sound begins again. Open juncture usually sets apart *words or parts of words;* level terminal usually sets apart *word groups or syntactical elements* within a sentence. Before the voice cutoff at these two junctures, there may be an appreciable prolongation of sound; in level terminal this prolonging action is slower, and more noticeable than in open juncture.

In two of the terminal junctures, a fading or trailing off of the voice accompanies a pitch change; in one, the pitch rises slightly as the sound fades; in the other, the pitch falls slightly as the sound fades. I have called the one fade-rise / ⟋ /, the other fade-fall / ⟍ /. The prolongation of sound is a little slower in these than in level terminal.

Depending on the general rate of speech, a "pause," or stretch of silence, may or may not follow a juncture or terminal before the sound begins again. In slow speech there are more of these intervals and they are more obvious than in rapid speech; in slow, deliberate reading aloud, pauses are usually quite noticeable. Yet the termination itself has occurred before the silence; it is an alteration and conclusion of the voice sound; its work is done and it is gone before any "pause" can occur. Thus to think of the termination and the succeeding silence as substantially the same thing is a mistake. The pause—if there is a pause—is simply an interval of silence. It is not much of a signal; it is rather a variable characteristic of style and rate in speaking or reading aloud.

We have seen that terminals and junctures are ways of patterning language by breaking or stopping the flow of speech sound, and that each specific terminal or juncture is a specific combination of pitch and manner of cutting off the sound. In successful reading, automatic memories of these interruptions should systematically "punctuate" the graphic counterparts of language patterns, such as sentences and paragraphs, reminding the ear of native melodies, or tunes. The fade-fall terminal has already been illustrated as used in simple statements, questions, and requests. Because it is clearly signaled by the period, often by the semicolon, and frequently by the question pattern and mark, it is most useful in teaching sentence sense in reading and writing. Normally this is a sentence-concluding terminal preceded by a one-level drop in the pitch contour, and normally should be heard only once—at the end—in an oral reading of any sentence-level utterance that is not divided by a semicolon.

Typically, the semicolon signals a fade-fall terminal, marked by a falling arrow / ➘ /—orally, the end of an utterance— though sometimes in an oral reading the level terminal may signify the separation of clauses by a semicolon. In a level terminal, the voice pitch at the "cut" stays at the same level as the tone immediately following the cut: level or sustained / ➞ /. An example like the following may be read with a fade-fall terminal at the semicolon, or with a level terminal, but probably with a slightly different intent, or attitude.

PRINTED: **John walked; Harry rode.**   (Two neutral statements,
pitch   minimally related)
contour
SPOKEN: **John walked** / ➘ /   **Harry rode** / ➘ /

PRINTED: **John walked; Harry rode.**
(More closely related, possibly with
pitch   an ironic or other suggestion)
contour
SPOKEN: **John walked** / ➞ /   **Harry rode** / ➘ /

Intonation: the melodies of the printed page   63

The level terminal may be considered an optional variant, in certain patterns, of the fade-fall terminal commonly signified by a semicolon. Somewhat like the question of special intent, it is interpretive rather than obligatory. I conclude that the level terminal is an intonation feature sometimes heard at the end of a sentence-level utterance in speech and oral reading, but not reliably signaled by graphic means alone.

We have now seen that two of the terminals commonly heard in American speech are frequently represented by punctuation in writing and print: the fade-fall terminal / ⟶ / and the fade-rise terminal / ⟋ /; they are commonly preceded by a one-level fall or a one-level rise in the pitch contour of the entire pattern. The level or sustained terminal / ⟶ / is a less significant cut in speech and oral reading; sharp but perceptible, usually it marks structural elements, such as noun groups, verb groups, prepositional phrases, or clauses. Because it is not graphically represented in writing and print by any specific symbol, in reading it often seems to inhabit a gray area between obligatory intonation and interpretation.

In certain patterns, however, the sustained-level terminal contrasts with the fade-rise terminal so as to indicate structure and determine meaning; the distinction between restrictive and nonrestrictive clauses is perhaps the most important instance; examples will be presented and discussed later in this chapter. The open juncture was introduced earlier, in connection with distinctive contrasts between such pairs as "I / + / scream" and "ice / + / cream," and the fade-rise terminal in counting and in series; the children's game song of "O'Leary" was introduced to suggest early mastery of this linguistic structure.

After the series and counting intonations, perhaps the next most common use within sentences of the fade-rise terminal / ⟋ /, commonly preceded by a one-level rise in the pitch contour, is to signal the end of an introductory phrase or clause in a sentence. The entire intonation pattern is characterized by a medium or heavy stress and a rising pitch, usually followed by a return to normal (the general pitch of the sentence), and on the last syllable or vowel sound before the interval, a slight rise again / ⟋ /. This gross pitch contour before the interval may be visualized as a large circumflex; the slight rise before the silent interval is the fade-rise terminal.

PRINTED: **After the rain, we played ball.**

pitch
contour   n———n——⌒n   n————n⌒‿

SPOKEN: **After the rain** / ⤳ /   **we played ball** / ⤳ /

PRINTED: **At my party, my mother served refreshments.**

pitch
contour   n— —n⌒‿n

SPOKEN: **At my party** / ⤳ /   **my mother served**

—n⌒‿
refreshments / ⤳ /

The clauses of a compound sentence are also commonly related to each other by a fade-rise terminal. The significant gross characteristic of the pitch contour, even in the "circumflex" pattern, is the rise above the general pitch level preceding the fade-rise terminal itself:

PRINTED: **I wrote a letter, but my brother went swimming.**

pitch
contour   —n⌒‿n

SPOKEN: **I wrote a letter** / ⤳ /

——n⌒‿
but my brother went swimming / ⤳ /

PRINTED: **She danced, but I studied my lessons.**

pitch
contour   n⌒‿n   —n⌒‿

SPOKEN: **She danced** / ⤳ /   **but I studied my lessons** / ⤳ /

Intonation: the melodies of the printed page   65

The elementary patterns above are basically the same as the more mature and complex sentences encountered in advanced grades and in later life. The learner who masters them during his basic reading instruction will not have trouble with them later on.

Generally, the fade-rise terminal (often preceded by a pitch rise to a higher level and return to, but not below, normal pitch level) occurs when the speaker or writer intends to signal that whatever language pattern he is closing is not the whole structure: the utterance *continues immediately.* This pattern occurs in series of all kinds, including compound sentences with more than two clauses; sentences with compound subjects or compound predicates in series of three or more; or, in any series of syntactical or grammatical structures within a sentence.

PRINTED: The boys gathered fuel, the girls set the table, and the parents were honored guests.

SPOKEN: The boys gathered fuel / ↗ / the girls set the table / ↗ / and the parents were honored guests / ↘ /

PRINTED: The boys, the girls, and the parents all enjoyed their summer picnic.

SPOKEN: The boys / ↗ / the girls / ↗ / and the parents / ↗ / all enjoyed their summer picnic / ↘ /

PRINTED: The picnickers gathered in fuel, set the table, and ate heartily.

SPOKEN: The picnickers gathered in fuel / ↗ / set the table / ↗ / and ate heartily / ↘ /

66   *Linguistics and the teaching of reading*

PRINTED: They searched in the woods, among the bushes, along
           the fence rows, and on the lake shore.

SPOKEN: They searched in the woods / ⟋ / among the
           bushes / ⟋ / along the fence rows / ⟋ / and on
           the lake shore / ⟍ /

PRINTED: Summer or winter, rain or shine, morning, noon, or
           night, they played cards.

SPOKEN: Summer or winter / ⟋ / rain or shine / ⟋ /
           morning / ⟋ / noon / ⟋ / or night / ⟋ / they
           played cards / ⟍ /

PRINTED: They went tobogganing every weekend, come wind,
           come snow, come rain, come sleet.

SPOKEN: They went tobogganing every weekend / ⟶ /
           come wind / ⟋ / come snow / ⟋ / come
           rain / ⟋ / come sleet / ⟍ /

PRINTED: May your loves be lyric, your health dramatic,
           Your tenor, in general, light-operatic.[1]

SPOKEN: May your loves be lyric / ⟋ / your health
           dramatic / ⟋ /
           Your tenor / ⟋ / in general / ⟋ /
           light-operatic / ⟍ /

Now you have seen examples of the main high-frequency uses of
the internal syntactical fade-rise terminal in relation to the
American English graphic system. Commonly preceded by a
rising pitch contour, it is highly relevant to the teaching of reading and writing at all levels.

Intonation: the melodies of the printed page   67

In speech and oral reading, the simple cut designated a level or sustained terminal / → / may be either an optional or an obligatory intonation feature, depending on structure and meaning. In reading, if the grosser intonation features already discussed are under control, this graphically unmarked terminal will normally be recalled where needed as part of the overall intonation contour of sentence-length utterances. A very useful distinction, however, that between restrictive and nonrestrictive clauses, may be signaled by the choice of a sustained-level terminal or a fade-rise terminal.

RESTRICTIVE: **My friend who sat next to me has moved.**

This sentence may be spoken or read aloud, without paralinguistic or interpretive features, in four ways, as follows.

My friend / → / who sat next to me / → / has moved / ↘ /
(Normal reading)

My friend who sat next to me has moved / ↘ /
(Rapid reading)

My friend / → / who sat next to me has moved / ↘ /
(Less rapid reading)

My friend who sat next to me / → / has moved / ↘ /
(Less rapid reading)

This sentence may also be punctuated, and either read aloud or spoken, so as to signal that the clause is NONRESTRICTIVE.

PRINTED: **My friend, who sat next to me, has moved.**

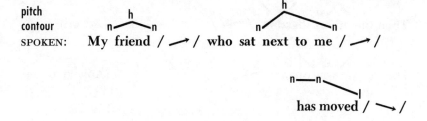

pitch contour

SPOKEN: My friend / ⟋ / who sat next to me / ⟋ /

has moved / ⟶ /

A slow and deliberate reading should produce a rising tone or circumflex pattern, as well as an appreciable interval, at the points indicated above by a rising arrow / ⟋ /. This rather fine structural distinction is of more practical use to teachers, no doubt, than to most children in school. When writing such a sentence, to determine whether the clause is restrictive or non-restrictive, *the important question is whether or not it can be read without terminals*. If it can, then the clause is restrictive (unpunctuated); on the other hand, if it requires the fade-rise terminals to convey the intended meaning, the clause is non-restrictive (set off by commas). Some speakers, however, use fade-falls in place of fade-rise terminals in such patterns.

It is difficult to know just how detailed a discussion of grammatical patterns of pitch, stress, and junctures and terminals is required by parents, teachers, and others who share in the excitement of introducing children to the graphic system of their mother tongue. Stress differences, used unconsciously by native speakers, distinguish a great variety of grammatical and syntactical structures. A particularly interesting feature of stress differences is their common use to contrast various structural positions and uses of what would otherwise sound like "the same word." For example, listen to the different degrees of loudness (stress) contrasting the structure of *in* distributed as a preposition, and in adverb and adjective positions in the following sentences. (A summary of the four stress symbols is at the bottom of page 71.)

Mary dived in the pool. / ⟶ /   (Preposition)

∧ ᴜ ＼ ／
Then the others dived in. / ⟶ /   (Adverb)

∧ ＼ ᴜ ／ ᴜ
The in gate was open. / ⟶ /   (Adjective use)

Similarly, in the following sentences, hear the contrasting stresses of *skin,* patterning in sentences in noun, verb, adjective, and adverb positions.

ᴜ ∧ ＼ ᴜ ／
The bear skin was huge. / ⟶ /   (Noun use)

ᴜ ＼ ᴜ ∧ ᴜ ᴜ ＼ ᴜ ／
There's more than one way to skin a cat. / ⟶ / (Verb use)

ᴜ ＼ ∧ ＼ ᴜ ᴜ ／ ᴜ
The toad's skin texture was pebbly. / ⟶ /   (Adjective use)

∧ ᴜ ᴜ ᴜ ＼ ／
Beauty's only skin deep. / ⟶ /   (Adverb use)

Moreover, stress differences commonly make subtler distinctions than those we have been listening to in the above examples. Most speakers will automatically differentiate *the White House, the white house,* and *the White house:* note that capital and lower case letters graphically signal the distinctive differences among the three stress-pitch patterns.

You have now seen examples of the four significant levels of pitch—**low, normal, high, highest**—and have observed a few of their relations to the terminals that mark the tip ends of the voice stream in structural sentence elements. These are the *level terminal,* indicated by the level arrow / ⟶ /, and the *fade-rise* and *fade-fall terminals,* indicated by the rising arrow / ↗ /

and the falling arrow / $\searrow$ /. The other juncture is the "internal" or open juncture, indicated by the plus sign / + /; it is a sharp cut that may separate words and syllables in clearly articulated speech and oral reading, but in itself is unrelated to either pitch or stress levels.

It now remains to summarize and present the four distinctive degrees of stress, in a classical linguistic illustration. We begin with heavy stress, because it is the stress of greatest importance, and because native speakers pick it up quickly; at this point we omit the other three degrees, because Americans vary considerably in their consciousness of them, and also because conscious mastery of all four is not needed for reading instruction anyway.

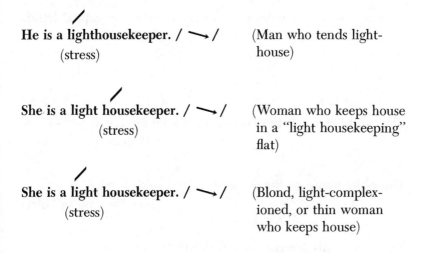

He is a **lighthousekeeper.** / $\searrow$ /   (Man who tends light-
   (stress)   house)

She is a **light housekeeper.** / $\searrow$ /   (Woman who keeps house
     (stress)   in a "light housekeeping"
                                    flat)

She is a **light housekeeper.** / $\searrow$ /   (Blond, light-complex-
   (stress)   ioned, or thin woman
                                   who keeps house)

Anyone can say these sentences with the distinctive intonations: stress, plus a rising pitch, on the marked syllables.

The four degress of stress—*relative* stress—are: the heavy stress (/), illustrated above, the medium stress / $\wedge$ /, the light stress / $\searrow$ /, and the weak stress / $\cup$ /. Here are the same sentences as before, but now marked for all four stresses. Note that all use the obligatory final fade-fall terminal / $\searrow$ /.

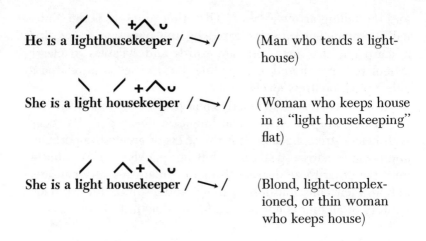

He is a lighthousekeeper / ⟶ /   (Man who tends a light-house)

She is a light housekeeper / ⟶ /   (Woman who keeps house in a "light housekeeping" flat)

She is a light housekeeper / ⟶ /   (Blond, light-complex-ioned, or thin woman who keeps house)

Now try the three *houses* we marked earlier by capital letters alone for heavy stresses, this time with stresses marked on both words.

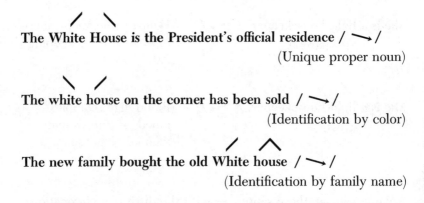

The White House is the President's official residence / ⟶ /
(Unique proper noun)

The white house on the corner has been sold / ⟶ /
(Identification by color)

The new family bought the old White house / ⟶ /
(Identification by family name)

If the above examples are easy and obvious, make use of them; but if the fine points elude you, don't worry about them. The main thing is to be able to locate the medium and heavy stresses, often associated with a rising pitch, and in general to realize that while four distinctive degrees of stress exist in the intonation system, you do not have to be *conscious* of them all at all times in order to use them properly. If your oral reading is fluent and easy, it will serve as a good example for children to follow.

The foregoing has not been a full linguistic description of American English intonation, but rather a functional presentation of primary and distinctive features of intonation that the eye should recall to the mental ear in reading; these features are of practical and immediate value in teaching reading as a language process. I have tried to suggest to the native American speaker a number of ways he may attune his eye, so to speak, to catch the graphic clues to these structural signals of intonation, so that in oral as well as silent reading, the patterns emerge consciously for him as melodies of the printed page.

It is not suggested or implied that silent reading should go at the rate of oral reading or speech. Quite the contrary. The rapid reader, like a music master, may take in large passages or whole compositions very quickly, and without a sound. But *what he takes in must accurately follow the form and structure the original creator traced in graphic symbols on the page.* Just as the musician does not read score or play music note by note, laboriously, the good reader does not read word by word, nor even phrase by phrase, but swiftly, freely, by entire language structures envisioned as wholes. His grasp of overall meaning is integral with his grasp of the whole language structure, because the language structure embodies the meaning designed by the writer.

Matters of intonation will come up from time to time throughout the rest of this book, because, as I hope is now clearly evident, intonation is basic to our language. Its features are always and everywhere a part of the grammatical and syntactical structuring of American English; as we successively explore word order, function order, and word groups, structure words, word-form changes, word formation and word analysis, I shall mention specific intonational features that characterize these structures. It is my deliberate method to proceed from the larger structure of sentence-level utterances, step by step, down through the component elements to that speech atom, the phoneme. I believe that this is the most fruitful approach for learning and teaching the graphic system of the already-known mother tongue.

In concluding this presentation of linguistic melodies of the printed page, it may prove instructive and amusing to illustrate the possibilities of sharpening the ear for intonation by occasional attention to simple paralinguistic, or interpretive, aspects of everyday language patterns. For example, the sentence *"I did not say you stole my red bandana"*—if it is to make sense to native speakers—must be read with the intonation feature that signals finality, the fade-fall terminal. There will also be a medium to heavy stress on *bandána,* usually accompanied by a falling pitch level preceding the voice terminal. But this simple declaration can be given as many different interpretations as there are words in it by using a heavy stress and a rising pitch on each word in turn—pitch may rise to high or highest level, or to "overhigh," depending on dramatic intensity—and by marking each word by a fade-rise terminal followed by an appreciable interval of silence—a "pause."

—hh
I / ⟋ / did not say you stole my red bandana.

                                   (Someone else said it)

  —hh
I *did* / ⟋ /   (Disputatious denial)

    —hh
I did *not* / ⟋ /   (Disputatious denial)

      —hh
I did not *say* / ⟋ /   (I implied, or suspected)

        —hh
I did not say *you* / ⟋ /   (Someone else stole it)

           —hh
I did not say you *stole* / ⟋ /   (You did something else with it)

              —hh
I did not say you stole *my* / ⟋ /

                                   (You stole someone else's)

                       ─hh

I did not say you stole my *red* / ⟋ /

                                 (You stole one of another color)

                        hh

                 n─

I did not say you stole my red *bandana* / ⟍ /

                               (You stole something else red)

This crude example does not begin to approach the interpretive subtleties our great language is capable of. Its virtue lies in being obvious; it illustrates various possibilities of interpretation without being ambiguous. Moreover, since these variations can be suggested graphically by underlines in writing, and by italic or bold face type, they are especially pertinent to reading and writing instruction.

CHAPTER FIVE

*Sentence patterns,
function order,
word groups*

the previous chapter, "The Melodies of the Printed Page," introduced the primary large sound patterns of American English from the point of view of reading and reading instruction: intonation is the organizing and integrating principle of the sentence, spoken and written. Speech and writing patterns are different in many ways, but they are closely and systematically alike, also. Opening out the discussion now, pursuing the native-language teaching method of proceeding from larger structural patterns to smaller, we take up sentence function order and word groups in this chapter, structure words in Chapter 6, word-form changes in Chapter 7, and word analysis in Chapter 8.

But in one sense we must discuss them all, or refer at least in passing to almost all levels simultaneously. The language system is a totality; we hear it, speak it, and respond to it all of a piece and all at once. The aim of reading instruction is to approximate this totality of intake visually, through mastery of the mnemonic graphic system. Because the readers of this book are native speakers, familiarity with the native tongue is taken for granted as a basis for both theory and practice. This chapter concentrates on four important sentence patterns, on function order and word groups, with only that minimum of reference to structure words and word-form changes that the presentation seems to require. There is no need at this point for any phonemic word analysis at all.

Four important sentence patterns

In visual or silent reading, just as in speech and oral reading, word order provides one of the most reliable clues to the total meaning-bearing pattern. In reading, children should be explicitly taught to begin at the left and move to the right across the page, rhythmically, by word groups and structure patterns, never literally line by line, for this often means senselessly breaking patterns at line-ends. The prescribed order of our graphic system must be patiently taught: left to right, back left and down a line, left to right, back left and down a line, always following the structures of the language system, rhythmically and fleetingly. This seeming correspondence of the graphic to the spoken form of language is an arbitrary convention, no more reasonable than our culturally determined customs of dress, or schedules for eating and sleeping. Just as reasonably, it might have been right to left, or top to bottom, or bottom to top, as it is in various graphic systems of other languages. For us, the main point is to read by *language patterns that carry meaning.*

Basic American English word order is quite rigid and arbitrary, despite its capability of a great variety of sentence constructions. Sentence variety is achieved almost exclusively through expansion and substitution within essentially rigid grammatical and syntactical structures; these structures may also be varied by inversion and systematic transformations. For reading instruction, word order is really quite simple. It should be taught to children at the earliest possible point in their learning to read, or remedially, at any time when they have not yet mastered it. A child who thoroughly learns sentence function order in familiar sentence patterns will not become a word caller, or a reader of disconnected structural fragments; instead, he will develop strong sentence sense.

The best method would be to teach the child to read and write the language patterns he brings to school with him. A danger of this "experience chart" method, however, is that artificial patterns reflecting vocabulary methods of teaching may be forced upon him by the teacher. *Let him first learn to read and write his own patterns,* "corrected" only in so far as necessary to bring them in line with the common patterns of sentence functions and word order as they have been described by linguists.

Before proceeding further in our discussion of word and function order in sentence patterns, it may be well to differentiate two fundamentally different species of words, or vocabulary, if you like: "full" words and "empty" words. Full words are clues mainly to content, to referents in the world outside of language; empty words are clues mainly to structure.

The great bulk of our vast English word hoard is made up of full words, words that call to mind some fairly definite referent, such as *banquet, dine, delicious, sociably.* But the most frequently used words are the relatively few empty words, or words having mainly structural meaning, like *the, up, down, when, because.* We have well over a half million full words, and the number constantly increases, at jet speed; we have only about three hundred structure words, and they increase with glacial slowness, largely through a shifting from full to empty word functions. Some empty words, in fact, retain traces of the meanings they carried when they were full words.

Full words may be conveniently grouped according to the four word classes, NOUN, VERB, ADJECTIVE, ADVERB; in this discussion, however, these classes are defined structurally in sentence patterns, according to their distribution. Empty words may readily be grouped in sets and understood according to the grammatical and syntactical functions the sets perform: NOUN MARKERS, VERB MARKERS, PHRASE MARKERS, CLAUSE MARKERS, QUESTION MARKERS, SENTENCE CONNECTORS, for example. Full words also give *structural* clues to sentence patterns and smaller pattern parts by their form changes and their obligatory syntactical positions; empty words, since their main significance is structural, provide specific signals for sentence patterns and smaller pattern parts. Reading instruction at all levels should take advantage of these important linguistic distinctions, which will be taken up more fully in Chapters 6, 7, and 8.

This chapter is particularly concerned with language patterns that carry meaning at the sentence level. Sentences in sequence within larger graphic structures (such as the paragraph) build up interrelationships into more complex meaning-bearing structures. In reading, the learner must grasp these meaning-bearing structures as wholes in order to comprehend meaning. Sentences are the basic building blocks of meaning: comprehension begins with sentence comprehension.

The historic model of the English sentence, and still the basic model, is the sentence with a "story line," having a time or action sequence. The "plot" may include *actor, action,* and *recipient* (or *consequence*); yet the simplest sentence has only actor and action, the traditional subject and verb. It is probably not an oversimplification to say that all English sentences are variations upon this one basic pattern: subject-verb. The "actor" may be a person or other living creature, a "thing," or an abstraction, idea, or concept.

ACTOR-ACTION	ACTOR-ACTION-RECIPIENT
A learner learns.	A learner learns arithmetic.
The radio works.	The radio receives broadcast signals.
Beauty fades.	Beauty launched a thousand ships.

Action in this model must be extended to include "seeming" and "becoming," as well as "being"—all those linking verbs traditionally said to denote being or state of being.

The child is a learner.	The child grew literate.
The radio became noisy.	The radio smells hot.
Beauty is only skin deep.	Beauty seems important.

Normal word order in American English sentences thus incorporates two basic sentence functions: (1) NOUN FUNCTION and (2) VERB FUNCTION, in that order; there may or may not be (3) a PATTERN COMPLETER. Such a pattern completer, if there is one, may include one or more of the traditional categories, direct object, indirect object, object complement; completing a linking-verb pattern, the completer may include a noun, adjective, or adverb function; some patterns with other verbs may also be completed with adverb and adjective functions, as well as noun objects. Any sentence pattern may incorporate simple or complex features of (a) *expansion* within the functions or of (b) *substitution* of one substructure for another within the pattern—two devices that make possible a variety of sentences with a variety of meanings. Or sentences may be varied through (c) *inversion* and (d) *pattern transformation.*

The child who goes to school will usually have operational control in speech of at least four important sentence patterns, traditionally known as declarative sentences; he will also be familiar with patterns of requests, questions, and passive constructions. The pupil who first learns to read and write these important patterns in simple form should then be able to advance easily to more intricate variations, inversions, and pattern transformations. *In silent and oral reading alike, the child must learn to grasp the total structures that convey coherent meaning: there can be no comprehension of meaning without a grasp of entire structures that carry meaning, or lead to it.* These structures are usually "higher level" than single words; exceptions are single words functioning as sentences. Whatever his age or grade, a learner can demonstrate his grasp of structure by intelligent oral reading of any sentence—including one he has written himself— with one of the normal, high-frequency, or obligatory intonation patterns. This oral reading may be regarded as a sufficient test of the student's grasp of structure.

If, as a general rule, the child is to be taught to read and write the language patterns he already speaks and hears with understanding—if these are to provide his basic manual-graphic materials and practice—he may not require much structural terminology at the very start. But it would probably facilitate his mastery of the language, as well as his control of the graphic system, if he soon acquired a conscious understanding of NOUN, VERB, ADJECTIVE, and ADVERB FUNCTIONS as they pattern in the language all around him. He would not memorize abstract and unreal definitions of sentence functions, or of word classes, but would rather be led to observe inductively the common uses of words—their distribution—in meaning-bearing sentence patterns. In school he should become *conscious* of abstract sentence patterns, and learn to use simple formulas for them, because he already employs these abstract patterns *unconsciously* in his everyday use of language, "sending" and "receiving" meanings.

Successful application of the pattern formulas about to be presented depends largely on the sympathy and understanding of the teacher. Given the right conditions, children take to them as games to play; but the formulas should not be forced, nor merely learned by rote. They are abstract but functional patterns: they produce meaning-bearing sentences. Children should not be asked to recite them.

N—NOUN FUNCTION	V—VERB FUNCTION
A—ADJECTIVE FUNCTION	Ad—ADVERB FUNCTION

The first pattern is **N V** for **Noun-Verb,** the simplest pattern in English, and probably the basic pattern from which all others may be derived. It occurs only infrequently without an adverb or an adjective pattern completer. The "plot" of the **N V** pattern has only an "actor" and an "action." **N** represents the **noun function** and **V** the **verb function.** These letter symbols and word formulations are used throughout this explanation of sentence patterns. The symbol **Lv** denotes the verb in linking-verb patterns. In simple **N V** sentences, the functions are filled by single words or simple word groups, but in more complex **N V** sentences a variety of substitutions, expansions, inversions, and transformations involving both **N** and **V** functions may occur. Similar variations are possible for all the important sentence patterns in this presentation.

PATTERN: **N   V**   **N   V**

EXAMPLES: **Bob   plays.** / ⟶ /   **Ann   runs.** / ⟶ /

            Bob   swims. / ⟶ /   **Ann   skips.** / ⟶ /

Even these simple sentences involve the verb inflection / -s / selected by third person singular nouns, and the typical fade-fall terminal at the end of each sentence.

Two variants of the **N V** pattern complete this first pattern group: **N V Ad** for **Noun-Verb-Adverb,** and **N V A** for **Noun-Verb-Adjective.** Both occur more commonly in speech and writing than the simple **N V** pattern. **N** and **V** represent the **noun** and **verb functions; Ad** represents the **adverb function; A** the **adjective function.** Many variations of structure, and consequently of meaning, are possible with these patterns. The learner's grasp of meaning depends on his unitary grasp of total structures that carry meaning.

PATTERN: **N   V   Ad**

EXAMPLES: **Bob   plays   well.** / ⤳ /

Ann   skips   high. / ⤳ /

Another variant has another kind of verb that may be completed by an adjective; **N V A** for **Noun-Verb-Adjective.**

PATTERN: **N   V   A**

EXAMPLES: **The door   slammed   shut.** / ⤳ /

The kite   broke   loose. / ⤳ /

The second important sentence pattern to be presented here is **N V N** or **Noun-Verb-Noun,** one of the most common sentence patterns in American English. **N** and **V** and **N** represent **noun,**

verb, and **noun functions** in an arbitrary order of functions, **N V N**, that cannot be changed except by inversion or some transformation of the pattern, without a change in meaning.

PATTERN: **N   V   N**

EXAMPLES: **Bob   plays   ball.**   / ⟶ /

         Ann   feeds   Chip. / ⟶ /

         Bob   drinks   milk.   / ⟶ /

Here the verb inflection is kept, and the fade-fall terminal ends each new sentence, with a medium or heavy stress on the final noun, instead of on the verb as it is in the **N V** pattern.

The heavy stress usually occurs on the final word of the structure as a whole. *From the very beginning of reading instruction,* teachers should see to it that children read aloud with high-frequency native intonations. It is especially important that children read with only one medium or heavy stress for each terminal structure within the sentence. Otherwise, they will not learn to associate intonation patterns with their graphic counterparts; instead, they will learn to "call" words, with fade-fall terminals on single words, or on nonstructural pattern fragments, that do not bear meaning. Comprehension will founder. Grasp of meaning is integrally linked to grasp of structure; intonation gives the unifying configuration.

An important structural question needs clarification here. Such kernel sentences as **Bob plays** and **Ann runs** do not commonly occur in everyday speech and writing, and should be treated in reading and writing instruction only as introductory to their more common expansions and variations. **Bob is playing** and **Ann is running** are more familiar, where a verb group replaces the simple verb form. This verb group is clearly signaled by the verb marker **is,** and completed by the **-ing** verb form, traditionally called the present participle. The pattern is easy for a child to see and read, after the signals are explained to him. One clear explanation will last a lifetime, because the structural elements are always and forever the same; only the verb bases (or roots) change. Practice is the ticket.

The simple patterns **N V** and **N V N**, in common use, are varied as above, expanded by adverbs or prepositional phrases, or both. ***Bob plays every day*** and ***Bob plays ball after school*** are the familiar patterns in their complete form; so are ***Ann runs home*** and ***Ann drinks milk at every meal.*** The children know these as audio-lingual patterns; they must learn only their graphic counterparts. Patterns simplified below common usage should be used, then, only as means of introducing the common, more complex variations the children know before they come to school. Teachers should be careful to avoid infantilizing the children's language in reading and writing instruction. Rather let the children make purely *graphic* mistakes, which can gradually be eliminated. A parent or teacher has only to give an example of any sentence pattern *with his own words in it* to start the children filling out the pattern *with their own words.* Smaller children especially often throw themselves into the game with élan. They make fewer mistakes than the older children, or than adults, particularly adults who have learned their "grammar."

The third pattern in this presentation is **N V N N**, for **Noun-Verb-Noun-Noun.** This formula covers a large group of structure patterns, the two commonest having different meaning patterns, with contrasting verbs and contrasting relationships of the **N N** functions in the completer. The contrasting verbs are exemplified by *call* and *give:* the *call* group includes words like ***appoint, choose, consider, elect, name, nominate, think;*** the *give* group includes ***afford, allot, assign, bring, buy, cause, deny, do, envy, fetch, grant, guarantee, hand, lease,*** and so on. Some words, such as ***make*** and ***leave,*** may appear in either pattern. The double-N pattern completer—**N N**—represents several compound complements of traditional grammar; direct and indirect objects, objects with object complements, and other such familiar categories. Structurally, **N** and **V** and **N** and **N** represent **noun, verb, noun,** and **noun functions,** in a rigid and arbitrary function order that cannot be changed without changing the meaning, except by pattern inversion or transformation.

Here are examples of the **N V N N** pattern with the verb **calls:**

PATTERN: **N   V   N   N**

EXAMPLES: **Bob   calls   his dog   Spot.   / ⌁/**

               Ann   calls   her bird   Chip.   / ⌁/

A new structural feature used here is the noun marker, exemplified by *his* and *her.*

Below are examples of the **N V N N** pattern with the verb *gives.*

PATTERN: **N   V   N   N**

EXAMPLES: **Bob   gives   Spot   milk.   / ⌁/**
               (or, **his dog**)

           Ann   feeds   Chip   seeds.   / ⌁/
               (or, **her bird**)

A fairly common pattern variant of **N V N N** is **N V N A,** where an adjective word-form and function replace the third **N**: *He painted the boat blue; They drove him crazy; Carbohydrates made him fat; The new music left him cold.*

The fourth of the important sentence patterns to be presented here uses the linking verb somewhat as the equals sign is used in simple equations. Indeed, this pattern closely resembles an equation, as young learners readily understand. The linking verb **Lv** may be used to relate (or equate) two **noun functions,** as in

N Lv N; the first **noun function** and an **adjective function,** as in
N Lv A; or the first **noun function** and an **adverb function,**
as in **N Lv Ad.** In this linking-verb pattern with an adverb completer, the **adverb function** is usually filled by a prepositional
phrase rather than by a single word.

PATTERN: N   Lv   N

EXAMPLES: Spot   is   a dog.   / ⤳ /

            Chip   is   a bird.   / ⤳ /

PATTERN: N   Lv   A

EXAMPLES: Ann   is   pretty.   / ⤳ /

            Chip   is   yellow.   / ⤳ /

PATTERN: N   Lv   Ad

EXAMPLES: Bob   is   here.   / ⤳ /

            Spot   is   out.   / ⤳ /

                    More typical examples with
                 phrases in the **adverb function:**

            Bob   is   in the house.   / ⤳ /

            Spot   is   under the porch. / ⤳ /

Before looking at the traditional passive structural variations of these four important sentence patterns, and before varying them by substitution, expansion, inversion, and transformation, let us briefly review what we have seen.

FUNCTIONS: NOUN   VERB   PATTERN COMPLETER

PATTERN ONE: **A. N V   B. N VAd   C. N V A**

A.   PATTERN: **N   V**

   EXAMPLE: **Bob   plays.**   / ⤳ /

B.   PATTERN: **N   V   Ad**

   EXAMPLE: **Bob   plays   well** (or, **on the team**).   / ⤳ /

C.   PATTERN: **N   V   A**

   EXAMPLE: **Bob   arrives   hungry.**   / ⤳ /

PATTERN TWO: **N V N**

   PATTERN: **N   V   N**

   EXAMPLE: **Bob   plays   ball.**   / ⤳ /

PATTERN THREE: **A. N V N N   B. N V N N**
                       (contrasting verbs and pattern completers)

A.   PATTERN: **N   V   N   N**

   EXAMPLE: **Bob   calls   his dog   Spot.**   / ⤳ /

B. PATTERN: **N   V   N   N**

    EXAMPLE: **Bob gives Spot milk. / ⟶ /**

PATTERN FOUR: A. N Lv N   B. N Lv A   C. N Lv Ad

A. PATTERN: **N   Lv   N**

    EXAMPLE: **Bob is a boy. / ⟶ /**

B. PATTERN: **N   Lv   A**

    EXAMPLE: **Bob is strong. / ⟶ /**

C. PATTERN: **N   Lv   Ad**

    EXAMPLE: **Bob is here. / ⟶ /**

Language is a living thing. It is organic in structure and function. Isolated language patterns, selected as examples of structure, and lacking content and communicative purpose, are obviously artificial. But the sentences in this display do illustrate four important sentence patterns, in language that is familiar, not only to children, but to us all. Patterns begin to sound more alive when we introduce their variants. They sound more alive especially when we enlarge them by various types of expansion, substitution, and transformation. Their real life is in the spontaneous flow of speech itself on the tongues of native speakers.

Important pattern transformations

Another common pattern of statement is the traditional passive-voice sentence; this is a structural transformation of the active-voice pattern. The active pattern is probably the basic structure; the passive may be thought of as the variant. Familiarity with both is important in developing the skills of literacy. (The traditional terms *active* and *passive* are "meaning" categories. As technical terms they have no special relevance to structure as such; *active* and *passive* are introduced here for readers familiar with traditional terminology.)

Recall the **N V N** pattern as in **Bob plays ball** or **Bob plays the game.** By syntactical devices—inversion of word order, and the introduction of the verb marker **is** and of the phrase marker **by**—we produce the passive transformation:

The game is played by Bob. / ⟶ /

A familiar variant of this transformation omits the **by** phrase (of agency):

The game is played. / ⟶ /

If we use the symbol **vV** for this passive verb group and **by** for the preposition normally used in this pattern, we have two new formulas:

N vV by N   and   **N vV**

In the **N vV** transformation, there is a specific passive structure and meaning relationship between the **noun function** and the **verb function.** The **N vV** sentence must be both a semantic and structural variant of the base pattern, **N V N.** In formal traditional terms, in the passive construction a form of the verb **be** is followed by a past participle; in terms of meaning, the subject is said to receive the action of its own verb. Similarly in the **N vV** by N pattern, the passive meaning-structure relationship runs straight through the noun, the passive verb group, and the **by** phrase: this sentence also is a semantic and a structural variant of the base pattern, **N V N**. In traditional meaning terms, the **by** phrase expresses the agency of the action; in formal terms, the preposition is the structure word **by**. Just as each of the four important sentence patterns presented earlier must be taken in all of one piece, as a unitary meaning-bearing structure, so must each pattern variant, or pattern transformation. Otherwise there can be no comprehension of meaning.

Now recall two of the common **N V N N** patterns, with their contrasting verbs: ***Bob*** gives ***Spot milk***, and ***Bob*** calls ***his dog Spot***. By inverting the normal word order and introducing the obligatory verb marker **be** and phrase marker **by**, we produce three passive transformations.

N vV N by N   **Spot was given milk by Bob. / ⟶ /**

N vV N by N   **Milk was given Spot by Bob. / ⟶ /**

N vV N by N   **His dog was called Spot by Bob. / ⟶ /**

Common variants of these patterns omit the **by** phrase.

N vV N   **Spot was given milk. / ⟶ /**

N vV N   **Milk was given Spot. / ⟶ /**

N vV N   **His dog was called Spot. / ⟶ /**

Many elementary school children are familiar with these interchangeable sentence patterns and will enjoy playing a game of converting, or transforming, one sentence into another, just for fun, or in direct relation to reading-writing practice.

PATTERNS	EXAMPLES
N vV	The ball was hit. / ⟶ /
N vV by N	The ball was hit by Joe. / ⟶ /
N vV N by N	Ann was given medicine by the doctor. / ⟶ /
N vV N by N	Medicine was given Ann by the doctor. / ⟶ /
N vV N by N	The medicine was called poison by Ann. / ⟶ /
N vV N	Ann was given medicine. / ⟶ /
N vV N	Medicine was given Ann. / ⟶ /
N vV N	The medicine was called poison. / ⟶ /

Another important kind of pattern transformation incorporates the "anticipatory subjects" of traditional grammar—**There is, There are**—also called expletives. In strict and proper grammar, **There is** selects a singular-noun pattern completer, **There are** a plural. Many speakers follow **There is** with a plural of one kind or another, however, especially in casual speech; and even otherwise careful speakers do this after the contracted form, **There's**.

There is *a book on the table.*   There are *books on the table.*

There's *a book on the table.*   There's *books on the table.*

There is *sand in the box.*   There's *pancakes for supper.*

There was *a pirate with a peg leg.*   *Then* there were *six.*

It structures similarly in common patterns.

It is *snowy today.*   It is *cold outside.*

It was *a long, hard job.*   'Twas *brillig.*

It was *a long time coming.*   It's *just not that way.*

It's *not like that.*   It's *simply awful the way he talks.*

It's often precedes a noun clause: **It's** *not that I don't like him.*
It's *because he doesn't match the wallpaper.*
    Following is a generalized formula for linking verb patterns
with **there** and **it** as pattern fillers:

There (or It)   Lv   pattern completer

    As pattern fillers, **there** and **it** often function in inverted pat-
terns in sentences like those shown above, not only with *be* and
other linking verbs, but with full verbs as well. For example,

There *followed three days of rain.*   (There V N)

It *developed that we were wrong.*   (It V N)

In structural terms, and in accordance with the formulas so far presented in this book, we may generalize that **there** and **it** function as pattern fillers in English sentences so as to initiate a complex variety of patterns that are essentially transforms of the **N V** prototype, and of the **N Lv N** group. These transformation patterns may be formulated as follows:

There (or **It**)   V N (or V N N)

There (or **It**)   Lv N (or N N)   (or **Lv A**)   (or **Lv Ad**)

These transformed patterns may all be summarized abstractly as fitting one or the other of two generalized formulas:

There (or **It**)   V   **pattern completer**

There (or **It**)   Lv   **pattern completer**

Frequently in writing, particularly expository writing, these transformations of common patterns are further transformed by incorporation of passive verb constructions. For example, *There were evolved many new theories.* This pattern may be formulated as **There vV N.** Combine these possibilities of pattern transformation with those of expansion and substitution, and you begin to glimpse the nearly limitless possibilities of variety in English sentences.

For basic reading instruction, two points deserve note:

(1) The pattern fillers **There** and **It** initiate entire transformations that are essentially inversions of **N V** and **N Lv** patterns.

(2) The intonation pattern normally gives light or weak stress to pattern fillers, and the rate of utterance is light and rapid. In the **There Lv** transformation, a heavy stress usually falls within the pattern completer. In the **There V** transformation, a medium stress often falls on the verb and a heavy stress follows somewhere within the pattern completer.

Systematic pattern variations

Questions, commands, and requests may be thought of generally as structural variants of the common basic statements we have been considering. If we searched, we could probably find examples of variants for every pattern in this display, but for reading instruction, perhaps only the most common need be introduced, along with general principles of pattern variation. Since the structure signals are well understood by most primary children, questions, commands, and requests offer an especially good opportunity to teach reading, writing, and polite conversation almost simultaneously. Courteous questions and requests constitute much of the small talk of daily life, the familiar rituals that help lubricate and make comfortable our personal relations in social groups. Children enjoy and profit from classroom practice in these forms, and in the socially accepted complementary paralanguage and kinesics.

The most common signals for questions are question-marking words and inverted word order, the characteristic elements of the pattern variations. The simplest and easiest questions involve the inversion of nouns and the verb forms of *be* or **have,** followed in writing and print by a question mark. **N Lv** inverts to become **Lv N? N V,** to become **V N?** These questions are so short that they can easily be taken in at a glance, including the question mark. As noted in the discussion of intonation, they normally end with the fade-rise terminal. The terminal itself is often preceded by a one-level pitch-rise. Children should be taught to see the entire pattern at once, and to read it aloud with the familiar intonation contour: **Lv N? /** ⟋ **/ V N? /** ⟋ **/**

PATTERN		INVERSION	
N	Lv	Lv	N
I	am. / → /	Am	I? / ↗ /
You	are. / → /	Are	you? / ↗ /
He	is. / → /	Is	he? / ↗ /
She	is. / → /	Is	she? / ↗ /
It	is. / → /	Is	it? / ↗ /
We	are. / → /	Are	we? / ↗ /
They	are. / → /	Are	they? / ↗ /

PATTERN		INVERSION	
N	V	V	N
I	have. / → /	Have	I? / ↗ /
You	have. / → /	Have	you? / ↗ /
He	has. / → /	Has	he? / ↗ /
She	has. / → /	Has	she? / ↗ /
It	has. / → /	Has	it? / ↗ /

We   have. / —→ /   Have   we? / —→ /

They have. / —→ /   Have   they? / —→ /

Sentence patterns with the verbs *be* and *have* seem to be the only ones that commonly invert so simply and naturally.

Perhaps the best clue to the question pattern in language familiar to children is an initial question marker—a structure word or empty word—such as *why, when, where, who, what, which.* Question markers may be used to signal the opening of a variety of sentence patterns, the simplest involving the inverted **N Lv** and **N V** just presented. When question markers precede these patterns, the questions thus signaled are normally uttered with the fade-fall terminal. The terminal itself is commonly preceded by a one-level pitch fall. These contrasting statements and questions provide a fine opportunity to teach children the *contrasting intonation patterns* of the simple inversions of sentence patterns with the verbs *be* and *have* without question markers and the same inversions signaled by question markers. As we have seen, the simple inversion without a question marker normally ends with a fade-rise terminal. With a question marker, it normally ends with a fade-fall terminal.

Question marker Lv N? / —→ /

Who was N? / —→ /   Who was he? / —→ /

Who was she? / —→ /   Who was it? / —→ /

What are N? / —→ /   What are you? / —→ /

What are we? / —→ /   What are they? / —→ /

Sentence patterns, function order, word groups   99

Which are N? / →/   Which are you? / →/

Which are we? / →/   Which are they? / →/

Where is N? / →/   Where is he? / →/

Where is she? / →/   Where is it? / →/

Where was N? / →/   Where was he? / →/

Where was she? / →/   Where was it? / →/

These are basic questions, all short and easy for a child to see and learn to read aloud with his normal intonation patterns.

The most common question pattern for converting into questions those basic statements that use verbs other than *be* and *have* begins with some form of *do: do, does, did.* This question-marking auxiliary verb carries its own grammatical inflection corresponding to that of the verb in the converted statement, and the original verb takes its base form. This question, especially in its short form, normally ends with a fade-rise terminal.

When we designate the question-marking-auxiliary v, the basic pattern **N V**, as in *Bob plays,* becomes v **N V**, as in *Does Bob play?*

N V	v N V
Bob swims. / →/	Does Bob swim? / ↗/
Ann skips. / →/	Does Ann skip? / ↗/

Pattern two, **N V N**, becomes v **N V N**, as follows:

N   V   N   v N   V   N

Bob feeds Spot. / ⌒→ /   Does Bob feed Spot? / ⟋→ /

Ann drinks milk. / ⌒→ /   Does Ann drink milk? / ⟋→ /

Pattern three, **N V N N**, becomes **v N V N N**:

N   V   N   N

Bob gives Spot milk. / ⌒→ /

Ann feeds Chip seeds. / ⌒→ /

v   N   V   N   N

Does Bob give Spot milk? / ⟋→ /

Does Ann feed Chip seeds? / ⟋→ /

Similarly, **N Lv N**, **N Lv A**, and **N Lv Ad**, using linking verbs other than *be*, would pattern in the same way, with a form of the verb *do* as a question-marking auxiliary verb. The only common inverted question pattern with linking verbs like *feel, seem, appear, taste,* and *look,* however, is **N Lv A**.

N   Lv   A   v   N   Lv   A

Ann looks pretty. / ⌒→ /   Does Ann look pretty? / ⟋→ /

On the other hand, in **N Lv N, N Lv A,** and **N Lv Ad,** using a form of *be,* **N** and **Lv** may simply be inverted.

N Lv N	Lv N N
Chip is a bird. / → /	Is Chip a bird? / ↗ /

N Lv A	Lv N A
Ann is pretty. / → /	Is Ann pretty? / ↗ /

N Lv Ad	Lv N Ad
Spot is out. / → /	Is Spot out? / ↗ /

These examples are appealingly simple, but some of them do not use the language most commonly heard and said by children. Uncommon language sounds artificial and should not be used longer than necessary to teach graphic forms of statements and questions in basic reading instruction. **Bob is playing,** as noted earlier, is the pattern commonly used, not **Bob plays.** Moreover, **Does Ann play jacks?** does not mean at all the same thing as the common question, **Is Ann playing jacks?** The question with **does** would not mean **now** or **at the present time,** but something like **does she ever,** or **is she able to,** or **does she like to, play jacks?** These common patterns are a little more difficult to read at first, because they involve verb groups, with auxiliary verbs and inflected forms of verbs, rather than single verb forms. But most young children are familiar with these structures in speech; as quickly as possible they should be taught to recognize their graphic counterparts on the printed page. Natural language patterns should be used as far as possible, and the artificial avoided in all basic reading materials (beginning with the first experience charts). Otherwise, we fail to utilize the rich native language knowhow of the children; we confuse them, and may even make them skeptical of our teaching. We will surely make them skeptical of our teaching if we insist on language patterns that violate the common forms in the children's experience.

Patterns of requests and commands

Commands and requests differ from each other not so much in basic language patterns as in paralinguistic and kinesic characteristics. Both normally begin with the base form of the verb, though formal-courtesy words and phrases may mark the pattern variant as a request instead of an order or command. Such social rituals as *please* and *if you please* ordinarily make clear that the pattern is intended to be a request rather than a command, although in tea conversations these pleasant amenities often sheathe barbs. But the ironic conventions of polite intercourse do not have to be taught to children, at least not in school; they learn them soon enough in the normal course of social life. When the child goes to school, he is familiar with the basic patterns of requests and questions. The task of basic reading and writing instruction is to teach him the graphic counterparts, with pleasant opportunities for practice in oral language activities involving requests and questions, including oral reading.

Commands and requests are important in the relationship of parents and teachers to children, in giving directions or making assignments, for instance.

Please clean up your room. / ⌒➔ /

Ann, please clean up your room. / ⌒➔ /

Clean up your room. / ⌒➔ /

Will you please clean up your room? / ⌒➔ / (optional / ⌒➚ /)

Please go to the chalk board. / ↘ /

Children, please go to the chalk board. / ↘ /

Go to the chalk board. / ↘ /

Will you please go to the chalk board? / ↘ / (optional / ↗ /)

The child who has a dog may know the single-verb commands in common use. *Come. Fetch. Heel. Sit. Lie. Stay.* And the most important single command of all: *No.* Three of them, when used with *please* or *if you please,* or with the verb marker *do,* become requests, if not downright pleas, when addressed to people.

Come, if you please. / ↘ /
      Please come. / ↘ / Do come. / ↘ /

Sit (or sit down), please. / ↘ /
      Please sit. / ↘ / Do sit down. / ↘ /

Stay, if you please. / ↘ /
      Please stay. / ↘ / Do stay. / ↘ /

Converted to question patterns, they become more polite as requests, but in these uses paralanguage is of equal importance.

Will you come? / ↗ /
  Will you please come? / ↗ /

Will you sit down? / ↗ /
  Will you not sit down (or be seated, or have a chair)? / ↗ /

Will you sit down, please? / ⟋ /
   Will you please sit down? / ⟋ /

Won't you please sit down and stay awhile? / ⟋ /

And so on. Offering excellent opportunities for training in the common courtesies, these patterns may be used profitably in experience charts. Because of their many variations, requests and commands challenge the child to master graphic counterparts of common language patterns. They challenge him to be alert to their signals on the printed page.

Requests, orders, commands all often begin with the base form of the verb; normally a pattern completer follows.

Be careful. / ⟶ / Be quiet. / ⟶ / Watch yourself. / ⟶ /

Look out. / ⟶ / Get ready. / ⟶ / Be prepared. / ⟶ /

Take out the trash. / ⟶ / Erase the boards. / ⟶ /

Pick up your waste paper. / ⟶ /

One common pattern employs a verb group divided by a pattern completer, as in *Have the car washed.* The verb group consists of the verb marker *have* and the past verb form *washed,* traditionally called the past participle; the noun and its determiner, *the car,* come between the verb-group elements. Other examples follow.

Keep the boys and girls working. / ⟶ /

Let them go home. / ⟶ /

Get the assignment done. / ⟶ /

Have the floor swept. / ⟶ /

Start the fan going. / ⟶ /

In requests, questions, and orders, there is a rich variety of expressions for precise shades of meaning. This variety may be useful in many ways and at many levels of language instruction.

On your mark. / ⟶ /   Get set. / ⟶ /   Go. / ⟶ /

May I have that book? / ⟋ /

I'd like to have that book. / ⟶ /

I wish you would telephone me tonight. / ⟶ /

Won't you please send a wire to Mother when you arrive? / ⟋ /

Let's hurry up and finish so we can go home early. / ⟶ /

Would you mind changing the subject, please? / ⟶ /

How would you like to go take a big fat jump in the lake? / ⟶ /

Word groups

So far we have discussed several important patterns of the statement, a number of structural variants of those patterns, and the intonation patterns that provide unifying configurations for entire meaning-bearing sentence structures. We have also had occasion to mention noun markers, verb markers, and question markers as they occurred in the sentences we examined. Now it is time to look at some of the word groups, expanded from single nouns and verbs, that may function as nouns and verbs in the common patterns we have previously discussed. *Understanding the systematic structuring of noun groups and verb groups is more significant for reading and writing instructon than almost any amount of study of individual words that may fill these positions.*

Within basic sentence patterns, substitutions of virtually every kind of language structure commonly occur, especially at higher levels of reading and writing instruction. Single words, word groups, clauses, noun and verb clusters (structures that incorporate clauses)—all may occur in any of the functions. Even in primary reading and writing, verbals such as the traditional present and past participles and the infinitive are found in simple, natural patterns. Following are examples of substitutions in the language of young children: *Swimming is fun*—present participle as first N in **N Lv N** pattern. *I like to swim*—infinitive as second N in **N V N** pattern. *We enjoy dancing*—present participle in second N function in **N V N** pattern. *Beaten today is not beaten for good*—past participles in both N functions in **N Lv N** pattern. Adverbs also occur in both N functions in the same pattern, as in *Down is not out* or *Just once in a while is not very often.* One of the familiar rules of sandlot ball is *Over the fence is out,* where a prepositional phrase is the first N and an adverb the second N in an **N Lv N** pattern. Learners at all levels should develop versatility in sending and receiving a great variety of messages involving substitutions in the basic patterns and their variants.

To avoid the word-calling that leads to word-by-word reading, children should not be taught to read single words as though they were significant as carriers of meaning in and of themselves. In the skeletal statement, *Bob plays* (**N V**), there is no noun marker because the noun is a "proper noun." Most "common nouns" are preceded by noun markers or determiners: *The boy plays.* Moreover, as noted earlier, the usual pattern is *The boy is playing,* in which the verb group is identified by the marker *is.*

As shown in the chapter on intonation, there is a final fade-fall terminal / ➘ / at the end of the statement—frequently preceded by a one-level drop in pitch. There are also pattern-marking stresses on *boy* and on *playing*.

The boy is playing. / ➘ /

A noun group like *the boy* can be expanded by adjectives coming between the noun determiner and the noun itself: *the young boy, the handsome young boy, the handsome young Greek boy, the handsome young Greek-American boy.*
Expansions of patterns like the following may be used to illustrate variations of patterns.

Bob plays. / ➘ /

The boy plays. / ➘ /

The boy is playing. / ➘ /

The young boy is playing. / ➘ /

The handsome young boy is playing. / ➘ /

The handsome young Greek-American boy is playing. / ➘ /

The child learns that the noun marker points to a noun; it is a structure word that must be followed by a noun. Everything between the noun marker and the noun is included in a noun group in which the noun is called the "head" or "headword."
Similarly, the child learns that a verb marker points to a verb. A glance of the eye tells the reader whether *is* stands alone as a

linking verb, or marks a verb group, as in *is playing.* Other verb indicators, or markers, are the tense and number inflections of *be* and *have: am, are, is, was, were; have, had, has.*

The boy is playing. / ⌒→ /   The boy was playing. / ⌒→ /

The boys are playing. / ⌒→ /   The boys were playing. / ⌒→ /

The boy has played. / ⌒→ /   The boy had played. / ⌒→ /

The boys have played. / ⌒→ /   The boys had played. / ⌒→ /

Other common verb indicators are the tense and number forms of *get, make, start,* and *keep;* and the modal auxiliaries, *can, could, may, might, must, shall, should, will, would, ought to.* If children are familiar with them and want to play with them in experience charts, they should be encouraged to do so, with an explanation of the verb-marking function.

The verb group works as a unit in the sentence; it is spoken as a unit, heard as a unit, and understood as a unit—within the larger meaning-bearing pattern of the sentence. It should be read as a unit, *in oral reading with a medium or heavy stress on the head word,* according to the pattern.

Let us return once more to the **N V N** pattern. We have seen noun and verb groups fill the first **N** and the **V** functions in this pattern; now we need to examine briefly the parallel use of noun groups in the **N** complement position.

The boy plays a game. / ⌒→ /

The boy plays a good game. / ⌒→ /

The boy plays a very good game. / ⌒→ /

The boy plays a very good game of ball. / ⤳ /

The boy plays a very good game of kitten ball. / ⤳ /

The last two examples introduce a prepositional phrase after the head word in the noun group. Its marker is a preposition. This preposition leads to a noun that completes the noun group. This is a new kind of word group in our discussion, one very important for basic language instruction because it is so well known to children.

Prepositional phrases are well known and frequently used from childhood on. They are common in children's games and everyday conversations, often in contexts where they serve as statements in answer to questions. In such use they should be regarded as sentences, by the teacher as well as the children; both question and answer are usually spoken with a one-level pitch drop and the fade-fall terminal indicating completion, or finality.

Where is Robert? / ⤳ /   In the house. / ⤳ /

Where are your toys? / ⤳ /   In my toy box. / ⤳ /

Where is your toy box? / ⤳ /   In my room. / ⤳ /

When did you lose it? / ⤳ /   After the movie. / ⤳ /

Where is the man in the moon? / ⤳ /

                         In the moon, / ⤴ / silly. / ⤳ /

We noted in our discussion of the first basic pattern, **N V**, that prepositional phrases often fill the **adverb function** in the

If rhyme and rhythm are desired—and why not?—teacher and children can join in devising patterns like these:

I have a ball. / ⌢⤳ /

I took a fall. / ⌢⤳ /

My uncle's tall. / ⌢⤳ /

I climbed the wall. / ⌢⤳ /

Here the contrasting words take the same position in the pattern, and receive the one heavy stress in the overall intonation.

Also important is precise use of capital letters and periods, and avoidance of careless misuse in board work and experience charts, because those points belong to the graphic system the children are learning. One or two wrong impressions made at the ages of six to eight may proliferate into a lifetime of confusion and error in writing. Lesson: *A sentence always begins with a capital letter and usually ends with a period.*

One other important pattern for reading instruction is the clause. Introduced or signaled by such markers as **because, when, who, that, if, where, before, after, since,** and **so,** the clause is a word-group that may have all the pattern parts of a sentence, but functions within unitary sentence patterns as a structural unit. In an introductory position, it may serve as an adjunct of a whole sentence. **When the rain stopped, the game was all over.** Like prepositional phrases, clauses are commonly used in children's conversations as statements in answers to questions. They are not "wrong" in such use, but in time, elementary school pupils should learn to switch from this natural use of isolated clauses in dialogue to combining clauses in sentences.

Why did you run? / ↘ /   Because I was afraid. / ↘ /
                            (Compare, **I was afraid.**)

Does it hurt? / ↗ /   If I touch it. / ↘ /
                        When you move it. / ↘ /

When did you hit him? / ↘ /   After he hit me. / ↘ /

Will you go with us? / ↗ /   If my mother lets me. / ↘ /

How long have you been home? / ↘ /
                            Since Daddy went to work. / ↘ /

Such clauses are also familiar to children as parts of larger patterns, and as substitutes for single words and word groups in regular patterns such as N V N and N Lv N.

Because you are bigger than I am / → /
                        does not mean   you can boss me. / ↘ /

When we get home after school / → /
                            will be   soon enough. / ↘ /

If I can go / → /   is   a big if. / ↘ /

Just once in a while / → /   is   not very often. / ↘ /

Clauses may also be used in the introductory position in materials suitable for basic reading instruction.

When it rains, / ⟋ / we play inside. / ⟶ /

If your mother says you can go, / ⟋ /
                                    my mother will take us. / ⟶ /

Before you go to school, / ⟋ / stop at my house. / ⟶ /

Where you go, / ⟋ / I want to go too. / ⟶ /

Since it has stopped raining, / ⟋ / we can go outside. / ⟶ /

Each of these sentences may be reversed to end with the clause:
We play inside when it rains. One of the beauties of using
clauses and clause markers with primary children is that the
children know them in speech, and they offer almost endless
variety in simple, familiar sentence patterns. Clause markers, like
noun and phrase markers, are clues to whole structures and to
the connections and relations of total meaning-bearing patterns.
Just so they should be taught. The next chapter examines the
various kinds of structure words more systematically.

CHAPTER SIX

Structure words

After intonation and sentence order, the most important clues to reading language patterns of sentences are provided by the structure words, or "empty" words, of American English. Happily for reading instruction, structure words lend themselves to graphic representation and visual perception. Since there are probably no more than 300 of them in our over 600,000-word dictionary, they could easily be dealt with by sequential introduction in school programs. Actually, nearly half (about 45 per cent) of the words in two well-known basic "sight reading" word lists are structure words, or words that commonly function as structure words. Yet despite the crucial role of these words in signaling the syntactical structure of meaning-bearing language patterns, the compilers do not differentiate structure words from full words. Later in this chapter a breakdown of the Dolch and Fry lists into full and empty words is displayed; Dolch (1942) and Fry (1960) represent a significant period of reading instruction and the compilation of such lists.

The most important structure words for basic reading instruction are five sets that may be thought of as MARKERS of structural sentence elements. The term *marker* is structurally accurate and easily understood, even by young children. It should be introduced and systemically used in primary and elementary language arts instruction. The five sets of common markers, with a few illustrative examples, are:

1. Noun Markers—*a, the, some, any, three, this, my, few* . . .
2. Verb Markers—*am, are, is, was, have, has, had* . . .
3. Phrase Markers—*up, down, in, out, above, below* . . .
4. Clause Markers—*if, because, that, how, when, why* . . .
5. Question Markers—*who, why, how, when, what, where* . . .

You have seen occasional references to most of these sets of empty words in previous chapters. There follows an orderly discussion of them, one by one.

But first a cautionary note. Structure words, above all, are words that should never be taught in isolation, but always as they function in the language, in typical structural order and patterns. If children are first taught to read markers individually, as "vocabulary" items, calling each one singly with a primary stress, later they may not be able to read them in native intonation contours, with the normally stepped-down stresses of American speech. Such "word" teaching will keep the child from carrying his acquired speech tunes over to his oral reading; subsequently, in visual or silent reading, the mnemonic echoes from the printed page will not repeat the native intonation patterns for him. Thus intrinsic linguistic signals for important structural elements may be corrupted, or lost completely, through faulty reading methodology. If the markers are always learned in relation to the words and functions they signal, however, great improvement in reading and writing skills will follow. Mastery of the clues to sentence patterning given by these most common words, rightly understood in structural contexts, is truly a key to unlock meanings.

Noun Markers

These are also known as noun determiners. Perhaps the most familiar are the articles of traditional grammar, *a, an, the;* though many other words function as noun markers. Sometimes in oral reading, children read noun markers as single words in isolation, with a primary stress and a falling pitch, practicing an intonation that is not English, and often with it practicing the long vowel sounds in *a* and *the* under stress, as in the emphatic forms of these words. Thus, learners often confuse *the* with *thee;* and the noun marker *a* with the name of the first letter of the alphabet (or with the letter itself) and with the sounds associated with the letter—confusion worse confounded. Occasionally these markers are normally uttered with the so-called long-vowel sounds: when they pattern with maximum stress in special intonation patterns used for emphasis. For example, *I said ā kitten, not a whole litter of kittens.* Or, *Is this man thē Mr. Franklin D. Roosevelt Jones?* Otherwise, noun markers occur as weak-stressed elements of noun groups. Structurally, a noun marker may be said to *select* a noun to follow it, sooner or later, in the structural element it has initiated; the name *determiner* implies an obligatory relationship and word order within the unfolding pattern of the noun group. To a reader visually retracing the language patterns of someone, somewhere, who wrote down what he is reading, the noun marker signals a meaningful structural element that he should grasp as a whole, within the larger pattern of the sentence. *All markers identify structural elements as meaningful wholes.*

In basic reading instruction, children should be explicitly taught to recognize noun markers for what they are, and to read them in noun groups with the native intonation patterns. Following are sentences illustrating *a, the, one, another, my, your, this, that, two, our, their,* and *most* in noun-marking functions. Three of the sentences contain more than one noun group.

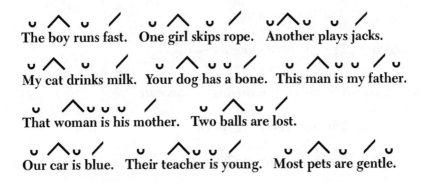

The boy runs fast.   One girl skips rope.   Another plays jacks.

My cat drinks milk.   Your dog has a bone.   This man is my father.

That woman is his mother.   Two balls are lost.

Our car is blue.   Their teacher is young.   Most pets are gentle.

As soon as they can, children should read noun groups with verbs, so as to associate complete spoken sentences and overall intonation patterns with what they see on the printed page.

Teachers can help the children associate audio-lingual with manual-visual experiences by preparing illustrative class materials for board work or for duplication on paper. In these materials, structural elements may be separated by spaces wide enough so that the children can readily see the word order within word groups, and the order and separate structures of the word groups within the larger patterns of sentences; but *the whole pattern should also be visually presented* in its usual form. And always the teacher should make sure the children understand that *whole patterns must finally be read as whole patterns.* No single word or larger structural element should ever be read as a finished structure, except, possibly, as a step toward immediate reading of the whole meaning-bearing pattern, with native intonation.

VISUAL: **The boy   is playing.**

           The boy is playing.

ORAL: **The boy is playing** / ⟶ /

VISUAL: **The girl   is skipping.**

           The girl is skipping.

ORAL: **The girl is skipping** / ⟶ /

VISUAL: **The man   is driving   his car.**

           The man is driving his car.

ORAL: **The man is driving his car** / ⟶ /

VISUAL: **The teacher   is writing   on the board.**

           The teacher is writing on the board.

ORAL: **The teacher is writing on the board** / ⟶ /

The principle of the noun marker also applies to larger and more involved language structures. *The boy* may expand to *the big boy;* then *the big tall boy;* then *the big tall handsome boy;* and so on. In intonation, the marker almost always receives a weak stress, and either the adjective or the noun receives a medium to heavy stress, while words before or after the more heavily stressed word take weaker stresses. We tend to speak the entire noun group at about the same rate, no matter how many words we add to it. *The big tall handsome boy is playing* and *The boy is playing* would normally be said in about the same time by the same speaker in the same circumstances.

In time, the child must learn that a noun marker may signal the beginning of a noun group with modifiers before the noun headword, and phrases and clauses after it, as well. Eventually, *The boy is playing* may become *The big tall handsome boy on our street who works at the gas station is playing.* Effective reading of sentences like this requires understanding of intonation, word order, and noun markers combined, and of verb markers, the next structure word set in this presentation.

Verb Markers

In traditional grammar, verb markers are known as auxiliary or helping verbs. In reading (or auding), verb markers signal, or provide clues to, the structure of the verb groups they introduce, contributing importantly to the delineation of whole sentence patterns. The common verb groups of American English, unconsciously so familiar to the native tongue and ear, have little to do with Latin-based verb paradigms found in school grammars. Teachers of reading and parents too, native speakers of the language all, should first become conscious of their own language practices, and then discover how these are graphically represented in print.

The most common verb markers for primary and elementary instruction are the forms of *be, have,* and *do.* The modal auxiliaries, so familiar in speech, are perhaps second in importance; they are *can, could, may, might, must, shall, should, will, would,* and *ought to.* Other verbs also function as verb markers; some of these are *get, go, start, keep, dare,* and *need.*

The three principal verb markers—*be, have,* and *do*—may also pattern as full verbs in their own right. Just as in reading noun markers as they pattern in complete noun groups, so intonation is important in reading verb markers as they pattern in complete verb groups; intonation provides the rhythmic clustering of words and the overall unifying configuration of the group. Both in full-verb and in verb-marking positions, *be* and *have* usually receive light to weak stress. In the following pairs of statements, the first example illustrates the verb-marking position and use of *is* and *has;* the second example, the full-verb.

˘ ∧ ˘ ╱ ˘
The boy *is playing.*

˘ ∧ ˘ ˘ ╱
The boy *is* his son.

˘ ∧ ˘ ╱ ˘╲˘
The youth *has graduated.*

˘ ∧ ˘ ˘ ˘ ╱ ˘
The youth *has* his diploma.

In oral reading, the marker in the verb group is distinguished from the full verb in the sentence by *visible grouping* of words in normal order and by *audible grouping* in intonation patterns. In silent reading, the mental ear should hear echoes of the normal tunes of speech, the melodies of the printed page.

In some uses, the auxiliary *do* retains an archaic flavor today, as in some of the old-time children's verses:

˘ ∧ ╲ ╱
Jack Sprat *does eat* no fat,

˘ ∧ ╲ ╱
His wife *does eat* no lean. . . .

Here *does* is a near relative of *doth* in modern form. *Doth* is an auxiliary and *have* and *do* are full verbs in the eighteenth-century nursery rhyme:

The north wind *doth* blow,

And we shall *have* snow,

And what will the robin *do* then, poor thing?

In its principal modern uses as a marker, the stress on *do* often gives assertive emphasis to the verb, as in such expressions of denial or contradiction as *I* did *practice,* or *I* did *come home right after school.* Parents and teachers will agree that these statements are not the same as *I practiced,* or *I came home right after school.* The marking function of *do,* but with more than a trace of special emphasis, is shown in the first of the following pairs:

The man *did try.*   The man *did* his best.

They *do attend* church.   They *do* what they can.

As a verb marker, *do* commonly differs from *be* and *have* in the stress-pitch patterns of the verb groups where it is used. This difference often signals special emphasis of some sort.

The verb *be*—as verb marker or full verb—has eight different forms: *be, am, are, is, was, were, being, been.* The verb *do* has five forms: *do, does, did, doing, done;* and *have* has only four: *have, has, had, having.* Verb markers may be used with other verbs and with their own full forms to produce a very great variety of verb groups. Consider the following examples:

The school *is being decorated.*

The classrooms *were to have been decorated.*

The classrooms *have been being decorated for weeks.*

Each student *has to study* at home. (Compare *must study.*)

Each student *has had to study* at home.

Each student *is having to study* at home.

Each student *had been having to study* at home.

Generally beyond what beginning pupils in reading are expected to be able to read, such sentences are common enough in the language. Children who master the reading of verb markers as signals of verb groups and grasp their patternings, both graphic and audio-lingual, will be prepared to read more involved structures when they do meet them.

Phrase Markers

Phrase markers are the prepositions of traditional grammar. Everyone knows a lot of prepositions. These structure words are important, especially in primary reading instruction, because they are so common and are used to form such a great variety of modifier groups. Prepositions are close relatives with adverbs; they call to mind a brown thrasher in a thicket: *up, down, in, out, above, below, beside, behind, around, along, across, from, to, by, with, into, near, on, off, through, toward, underneath, upon, outside, inside, within*—a flash of brown feathers, and gone *with* the wind. In reading instruction the lesson is the same for prepositions as for noun and verb markers: they signal, or provide clues to, structural word groups that in turn help delineate the larger structures in which they function. Prepositions usually receive weak to light stress. Both visually and orally, they should be perceived not singly, in isolation, but as starters of structural groups.

Prepositional phrases are excellent structures in work with experience charts. Children know many of them and the basic pattern is simple. Beyond learning to read and write their own language patterns, children can learn to set prepositions in opposition, and thus make early contact with a basic linguistic operation: contrasting forms. Consider the following phrases:

up the tree	*down* the tree
into the house	*out of* the house
in the window	*out* the window
above the ground	*below* the ground
over the fence	*under* the fence
inside the box	*outside* the box
for us	*against* us
after school	*before* school

In conversation, as noted earlier, phrases and other partial structures may be used occasionally as complete sentences. Generally, though, they should be taught as *sentence elements* rather than as complete structures, with weak to light stress on the preposition. Reading of isolated prepositional phrases may alter normal intonation patterns harmfully, if we want the children to associate their native tunes with written and printed counterparts. And we do.

Clause Markers

A clause is a word group with an **N V** pattern as its basic structure; this **N V** pattern, of course, is chiefly what differentiates a clause from a phrase. Clause markers are a set of structure words that have been given a bewildering and inconsistent set of names in traditional grammar: "subordinating conjunction," "relative pronoun," "conjunctive adverb," or "adverbial conjunction," "introductory adverb," "illative conjunction," and the like. These names are confusing and often a bit misleading, because the clause marker itself does not necessarily indicate the function of the clause in the larger pattern, where the clause may fill the position and function of a noun, an adjective, an adverb, or occasionally even a verb.

In general, a clause begins with a marker (a single word or a word group) signaling that a clause is about to unfold. This clause marker is the invaluable clue that children must be taught to pick up quickly in reading, eventually as if by instinct. If any one structure word in reading and writing is more important than the others, it is probably the clause marker, because prose tends to favor clauses, and the clause marker is capable of showing so many different kinds and degrees of structural relationships, which reflect myriad meanings. Relatively devoid of meaning themselves—empty—they illuminate involved structures of entire patterns, and so provide sophistication, depth, and structural richness to our language. Reading clause markers quickly and accurately in their functions is a first requirement of effective comprehension of meaning.

Children from five to seven are already familiar in speech with simple clause markers like *if, when, why, so, until, once, now, as, where, who, whose, what, which, before, after, like, than, though*—and probably many others. Some of these are also question markers; as question markers they have already been discussed in Chapters 4 and 5. To children who are struggling to master reading and writing, it is of greater help to teach them to recognize and use clause markers and other structure words than to teach them a vocabulary of full words. Language is best understood as a system of significant structures; single full words, though important, are not of the same order of importance as syntactical structures or as the structure words that initiate them and signal their approach. Significant structures easily acquire the words needed to fill them, according to circumstances and need. But full words are relatively insignificant in themselves, since they can function only in larger, structurally significant, meaning-bearing patterns; they can neither define structures themselves nor contribute much to structure. It is artificial, if not linguistically fallacious, to single out individual words from the structures that define their meanings. It has been argued that the definition of a word is simply its DISTRIBUTION in meaning-bearing language structures.

Some clauses occur without markers—often adjective clauses like those italicized in the following sentences.

The boy *you met at camp* is my cousin.

The ball *she bought yesterday* is lost.

The movie *I saw last night* was pretty good.

The team used the new equipment *we purchased.*

Noun clauses without markers also occur in common patterns.

I know *he had one in his pocket.*	N V N
Mother said *Priscilla was sick.*	N V N
We could tell *we were lost.*	N V N
It was so cold was why we were late.	N Lv N
Daddy guessed *it wouldn't work.*	N V N

Children should learn early to respond to the total pattern and recognize the functions of clauses and phrases within total patterns. Reading clauses aloud with appropriate rhythms and tunes will help develop sentence sense in both reading and writing.

Here is a list of the most common clause markers:

that, so that, in that, such that, in order that, lest

so, as, only, like, than

*when, where, why, how, whenever, wherever, however,
     whither, whence, whereby, wherein, whereof*

*who, whom, whose, whoever, whomever, what, whatever,
     whatsoever, which, whichever*

*if, whether, although, though, while, unless, except,
     notwithstanding*

*since, because, as, inasmuch as, whereas, seeing, being as,
     being that*

before, after, ere, till, until, once, now, as soon as, so long as

Question Markers

In Chapter 5 we discussed questions as variant forms of
common patterns of statement. Following is a list of the most
common question markers:

*when, where, why, how, whenever, wherever, however, whither,
whence, who, whom, whose, whoever, whomever, what, whatever, which, whichever*

Question markers occur commonly among the language patterns
of children.

When will supper be ready?

Where are my skates?

Why do I have to?

How can I, Mother?

Who is coming?

Whose book is this?

What do I have to do next?

Which one is for me?

Other Structure Words

A few other sets of structure words are important for basic reading and writing instruction: the conjunctions of traditional grammar, and *intensifiers*. There are also minor sets, "proposers" like those mentioned in Chapter 5, and "starters." Proposers are such expressions as *Please, If you please, If you don't mind, If you like, If it's no trouble, Would you mind, Be so kind,* and so on. Starters are casual expressions of everyday talk like *Well, Oh, Say, Look, Now, Why, O.K., Listen, See here, Bud, Listen Kiddo, Charlie, Mac, Children,* and all proper names designated in traditional grammar as the nominative of address. Since most of these are used and understood by young children, they require only an indication of their role in the basic patterns.

Conjunctions are a set of structure words serving as connectors between similar structures; the seven most common conjunctions are *and, but, for, nor, or, yet,* and *so.* Conjunctions may be used to connect two or more structures of any kind, single words, whole sentences, and even paragraphs. Generally, it is not good writing style to repeat the same patterns to the point of monotony, but there is no reason why sentences may not effectively begin with conjunctions. Children should be permitted, not forbidden, to use these words in any familiar ways in composition, beginning with experience charts.

Certain conjunctions, the coordinating conjunctions of traditional grammar, often work in pairs to signal certain significant structural relationships and meanings; in such structures, they are the traditional correlative conjunctions. The following listing attempts to range roughly from those pairs most common at the primary level to pairs less common.

both . . . . and	*as . . . . as*	*if . . . . then*
now . . . . now	*now . . . . then*	*so . . . . as*
either . . . . or	*neither . . . . nor*	*not . . . . but*
not only . . . . but	*not only . . . . but also*	*if . . . . still*
whether . . . . or	*when . . . . then*	*while . . . . still*
where . . . . there	*while . . . . yet*	
although . . . . yet	*although . . . . still*	

Some of these structural pairs occur only in formal writing, but many occur even in the speech of children. The children will read more effectively if their attention is called to the linguistic principle of correlative pairs of conjunctions as the occasion arises in their writing and reading practice.

Intensifiers are very common in the language of youngsters, reflecting the vivacity and keen feelings of childhood. Intensifiers occur before adjectives and adverbs, and intensifying endings occur after some familiar adjectives and adverbs, to sharpen the meaning; occasionally an "intensifier" in structure minimizes or reduces the intensity of meaning: **less cold,** for example. These are some of the most common intensifiers:

very, more, most, little, less, least

quite, awfully, awful, really, real, any, pretty, too, fairly

rather, somewhat, somehow, right, just, more or less, so

Intensifiers sometimes combine to form extended groups, as in **very much, very much more,** and **so very much more.** Several words serve as intensifiers before adjectives and adverbs with the *-er* inflection, such as **better, softer, harder, stronger, bigger, taller, fatter, shorter, older, younger,** and so on. A few of these intensifiers are **still, even, some, no, away, far, and away, much,** and——**times (ten, fifty, one hundred).**

At the beginning of this chapter we promised to present a breakdown into full words and empty words of two basic word lists for primary reading instruction—the Dolch Basic Word list of 220 "service" words and the Fry list of 300 Instant Words.

Below are the 220 service words as presented to the child in the Dolch Basic Sight Words Tests, Parts 1 and 2. Directions indicate the tests may be administered in either of two ways: (1) the tester reads one word from each line from a list on a scoring sheet, and asks the children to circle the word; or (2) individually, the child is asked to read aloud all the words, *line by line.*[1] (Words in boldface italics are structure words, or commonly function as structure words, including pronouns.)

PART 1

1. *by*   *at*   *a*   *it*

2. *in*   *I*   *be*   big

3. *did*   good   *do*   go

4. *all*   are   any   an

5. *had*   have   *him*   drink

6. *its*   *is*   *into*   if

7. ask   *may*   as   am

8. *many*   cut   *keep*   know

9. *does*   *goes*   going   *and*

10. *has*   *he*   *his*   far

11. *but*   jump   *just*   buy

12. black   kind   blue   find

13. fast   first   ate   eat

14. help   hot   *both*   held

15. brown   grow   bring   green

16. *four*   *every*   *found*   **eight**

17. **from**   *make*   **for**   *made*

18. **around**   *funny*   *always*   **because**

19. *long*   *let*   *little*   *look*

20. *away*   *again*   **after**   **about**

21. *cold*   **can**   **could**   *clean*

22. *full*   *fall*   **five**   *fly*

23. **before**   *best*   *better*   *been*

24. *live*   **like**   *laugh*   *light*

25. **her**   *here*   **how**   *hurt*

26. **down**   *done*   *draw*   **don't**

27. *give*   **get**   *gave*   **got**

28. *came*   *carry*   *call*   *come*

PART 2

1. *sit*   **me**   *to*   **the**

2. **not**   *of*   *we*   *so*

3. red   too   **seven**   walk

4. **six**   **start**   show   stop

5. put   round   right   pull

6. **no**   **on**   **or**   old

7. yellow   **you**   **your**   yes

8. **please**   pick   play   pretty

9. take   **ten**   **they**   today

10. **my**   **much**   **must**   together

11. own   **under**   **off**   over

12. **out**   new   now   **our**

13. open   **one**   only   once

14. try   **myself**   never   **two**

15. **us**   **up**   **upon**   use

16. **with**   white   **was**   wash

17. **shall**   **she**   sleep   small

18. **who**   write   **would**   why

19. *some*   *very*   sing   soon

20. *wish*   well   work   *will*

21. ran   read   run   ride

22. then   tell   *their*   *them*

23. see   saw   say   said

24. *that*   there   *these*   *three*

25. *when*   *which*   *where*   *what*

26. thank   *those*   *this*   think

27. want   went   *were*   warm

Dr. Edward Fry presented his 300 Instant Words in *Elementary English,* arranged in twelve groups according to the order of difficulty.[2] He reports that in classroom practice the words are presented by various means, including flash cards, tachistoscopes, card games, spelling lessons, and easy reading. (Words in boldface italics are structure words, or may function as structure words, including pronouns regarded as a subset of nouns.)

First Hundred Words (approximately first grade)

GROUP 1

the   *a*   *is*   *you*   *to*   *and*
we   *that*   *in*   *not*   *for*

at   with   it   on   can
will   are   of   this   your
as   but   be   have

GROUP 2

he   I   they   one   good
me   about   had   if   some
up   her   do   when   so
my   very   all   would   any
been   out   there   from   day

GROUP 3

go   see   then   us   no   him
by   was   come   get   or   two
man   little   has   them   how
like   our   what   know   make
which   much   his

GROUP 4

who   an   their   she   new
said   did   boy   three   down
work   put   were   before   just
long   here   other   old   take
cat   again   give   after

Second Hundred Words (approximately second grade)

GROUP 5

saw   home   soon   stand
box   upon   first   came   girl
house   find   because   made
could   book   look   mother

run	school	people	night
into	say	think	back

GROUP 6

big	**where**	**am**	ball	morning
live	**four**	last	color	away
red	friend	pretty	eat	want
year	white	**got**	play	found
left	men	bring	wish	black

GROUP 7

may	let	use	**these**	
right	present	tall	next	
please	leave	hand	**more**	
why	better	**under**	**while**	
should	never	**each**	best	
another	seem	tree	name	
dear				

GROUP 8

ran	**five**	read	**over**	**such**
way	too	**shall**	own	**most**
sure	thing	only	**near**	**than**
open	kind	**must**	high	far
both	**and**	**also**	**until**	call

Third Hundred Words (approximately third grade)

GROUP 9

ask	small	yellow	show
goes	clean	buy	thank
sleep	letter	jump	self

fly   **don't**   *fast*   *cold*
today   **does**   *face*   *green*
every   *brown*   *coat*   **six**
gave

GROUP 10

hat   *ear*   *write*   *try*   **myself**
longer   **those**   *held*   *full*
carry   **eight**   *sing*   *warm*   *sit*
dog   *ride*   *hot*   *grow*   *cut*
seven   *woman*   *funny*   **yes**
ate   *stop*

GROUP 11

off   *sister*   *happy*   *once*
didn't   *set*   *round*
dress   *fail*   *wash*   **start**
always   *anything*   **around**
close   *walk*   *money*   *turn*
might   *hard*   **along**   *bed*
fine   *sat*   *hop*

GROUP 12

fire   **ten**   *order*   *part*   **only**
fat   **third**   *same*   *love*   *hear*
yesterday   *eyes*   *door*   *clothes*
though   *o'clock*   **second**   *water*
town   *took*   *pair*   *now*   **keep**
head   *food*

Both the Dolch and the Fry lists were compiled from reading instruction books used in the first three grades; Dolch claimed that his 220 "service" words made up 70 per cent of first-grade readers and 65 per cent of the second and third grade readers; Fry claims that the Instant Words are the 300 commonest words in the English language, and that they make up 63 per cent of readers sold by three major publishers for the first three grades. Although the Dolch list is a long generation older, 200 of the 220 words are included in the Fry list. The language used by the authors of primary readers has not changed much within recent memory.

Dolch and Fry argue for sight learning of the individual items in their basic lists, without phonics instruction, which they believe is overdone, but neither mentions the structural functions of these little words in larger language patterns. The Dolch list contains no nouns; *107 words, or approximately 46 per cent, are structure words:* conjunctions, starters, intensifiers, pronouns, and noun markers, verb markers, phrase markers, and clause markers. The Fry list contains common nouns; *129 words, or approximately 43 per cent, are structure words;* Fry himself admits some difficulty in teaching them as vocabulary items *because they are "largely devoid of subject-matter meanings or object reference."*[3]

Neither Dolch nor Fry reveals an understanding of reading as a language-related process; to them, apparently, phrases and word groups are arbitrary segments of print having more to do with linear distance, possibly with eye span, than with meaning-bearing language structures. Both Dolch and Fry are primarily concerned with teaching isolated words—"vocabulary." Their experience with children and their native-language instincts lead them to a primitive language analysis of publishers' reading materials—word counts, without regard to structure or function. The methods these two compilers recommend for teaching their lists are the quintessence of concentration upon single words, disregarding language patterns that bear meaning. If such methods and materials are commonly used in primary reading instruction, is it any wonder that so many children later "read words" in patternless, meaningless sequences?

The next two chapters, 7 and 8, present the topics usually included under such headings as WORD ANALYSIS, WORD ATTACK, and PHONICS. Chapter 7 presents the four word classes, whose systematic form changes comprise the grammatical inflections of modern English; this discussion completes this exposition of the American language from the perspective of basic reading viewed as a native-language process. Chapter 8 discusses the relationships of the spelling system to the phonemic system of American English, proposes a linguistically oriented system of phonics, and outlines some important information about combining bases and word endings, fundamental to structural word analysis.

CHAPTER SEVEN

*Word-form changes:
the four word classes*

O f the four main devices of the American language system that are in some degree graphically represented in writing and print —intonation, function order in sentences, structure words, and word-form changes—only word-form changes, chiefly grammatical inflections, remain to be discussed in relation to reading. Modern English is a relatively uninflected language, compared to modern Russian or German, for instance; compared to its Old English ancestor of a thousand or so years ago, our language retains no more than a residue of an elaborate Germanic system of grammatical inflections. For signaling structural patterns, this residue is less important than intonation, sentence order, and structure words; yet the word-form changes we do have yield important clues to structure. Represented clearly in graphic form and clearly heard in speech, they are essential to reading instruction: word-form changes are spelled consistently regardless of the sounds they "spell." These grammatical inflections are structural elements of the four main word classes in English: NOUN, VERB, ADJECTIVE, ADVERB; full words with specific inherent pattern signals that readers must take in if they are to comprehend meanings. In addition to grammatical inflections, this discussion touches upon another set of word-form changes, the common derivational prefixes and suffixes.

So far in this book we have been considering only the larger features of entire meaning-bearing language patterns. Aside from intonation, the overriding feature of utterances, we have discussed patterns of sentence functions and have differentiated full words from empty words (structure words). At the point of analyzing the structural word-form changes that mark the four main classes of words, it may be well to clarify some pertinent linguistic distinctions. Concepts symbolized by the terms *sentence function, word-form class, distribution,* and *word use,* as they apply throughout this discussion, require further elucidation.

The terms *noun, verb, adjective,* and *adverb* may refer to both sentence functions and word-form classes; but these two structural categories are not the same and need not be confused. Class and function may falsely appear to be identical because single words may in fact fill sentence functions; the high frequency of expansions and substitutions in the functions, however, demonstrates the qualitative difference between word class and sentence function.

Many members of English word-form classes are marked by their ability to take the form changes—inflections, prefixes, suffixes—characteristic of the given class. But by this same test, many words belong to two or more form classes. Only the distribution, or position, of such words in larger patterns determines which class they belong to; no such word by itself can be said to belong to any single class. Another point of possible confusion is the fact that many words which do not and cannot take the class-marking form changes may nevertheless substitute in patterns for words that do; this kind of word substitution is what is meant in this discussion by the term *use*, or *word use*.

To sum up: (1) SENTENCE FUNCTIONS are qualitatively different from the WORD-FORM CLASSES that bear identical names: NOUN, VERB, ADJECTIVE, ADVERB. (2) Single words may belong to more than one class by virtue of their ability to take the characteristic word-form changes that mark classes; their DISTRIBUTION, or position in sentences, identifies the class in each instance. (3) Words of a given word-form class may substitute for words of another class—such substitution is a USE of one word as a member of the other class.

The most important part of word analysis, especially in basic reading instruction, is correct identification of word classes and their characteristic word-form changes, because mastery of language patterns at the sentence level is made easier by such identification. (Phonics aspects of word analysis will be presented in Chapter 8.) As we have seen, form-class membership determines neither distribution nor word use in English sentences. Many words cannot be assigned to any class except when they are seen or heard in a structural pattern. *Stone*, for example, may be inflected and distributed as either noun or verb, and thus belongs to both noun and verb classes; *stone* may also be used in adjective and adverb positions, but cannot take adjective and adverb form changes of comparison. Like many another noun, *stone* may take the adjectival suffix *-y*, in *stony*, which in turn may take the adverbial suffix *-ly* in *stonily;* these are derivational suffixes, however, unlike the grammatical inflections marking the four word classes as form classes. The derived adjective *stony,* of course, may take the comparative forms, *stonier* and *stoniest.*

The chaste wife dropped a large *stone* in the well.

(**Noun** form class)

The guilty all went out to *stone* the innocent. (**Verb** form class)

Excellent peaches may be grown against a *stone* wall.

(Adjective *use*)

For basic reading instruction it may not be necessary to understand the adverbial uses of nouns as in *stone* blind, or *stone* drunk (or simply *stoned,* a past participle in an adjective position). But these substitutions, ordinary and sophisticated, help explain why word order—actually *function order in sentence patterns—* is so much more important in reading American English than single words, or even word-form classification of single words. We should simply teach children to observe grammatical inflections for whatever they are worth, no more and no less.

In our language, a noun may be either singular or plural in form, generally speaking; a structural definition of NOUN is a word that can take the plural inflection. The regular noun plural inflection is spelled *-s,* and may be spoken three different ways, as in cat*s* / *-s* / (a hiss), dog*s* / *-z* / (a buzz), and horse*s* / *-iz* / (indeterminate, weak-stressed vowel, plus buzz). The noun plural inflection, its spelling, and its three different sounds should be taught early in reading instruction. The plural hiss / *-s* / is heard after unvoiced stop consonants / k /, / p /, / t /, and the unvoiced continuants / f /, and / θ /. Common examples are:

/ ks /   *books, marks, clocks, cooks, locks, blocks, bikes, cakes, rakes*

/ ps /	maps, tops, tapes, types, snaps, ropes, nips, naps
/ ts /	cats, rats, baits, boats, nights, wits, cots, nets, knots
/ fs /	whiffs, tiffs, miffs, pontiffs
/ θs /	myths, wraiths, laths, wreaths, plinths

The plural buzz $/-z/$ is heard after the voiced consonant stops, $/g/$, $/b/$, $/d/$, that contrast with the unvoiced stops, and the voiced continuants $/v/$ and $/ð/$. Common examples are:

/ gz /	dogs, rags, legs, rogues, tags, logs, pigs, pegs, bogs, pugs, mugs, rigs
/ bz /	cobs, robes, babes, bibs, nibs, fibs
/ dz /	lads, lids, brides, pods, rides, codes, hods, heads, needs, foods, hoods, broods
/ vz /	lives, waves, weaves
/ ðz /	lathes, withes

The plural buzz $/-z/$ is also heard as a plural inflection after nouns that end with long vowel sounds, with the liquids ($/r/$ and $/l/$), the nasal continuants ($/m/$ and $/n/$), and the sound usually spelled ng, $/ŋ/$. All are voiced. Common examples are:

/ eyz /	rays, plays, ways, yeas, nays
/ owz /	rows, snows, minnows, crows, blows, does, hoes, toes, potatoes, woes, foes, noes

/ ayz /	flies, sighs, cries, highs
/ uwz /	flues, moos, glues, screws
/ iyz /	fleas, teas, trees
/ lz /	balls, decals, holes, miles, pills, tales
/ rz /	cars, stars, bars, mars, cures, floors, moors, years, tears, peers, cares, wares, pears, chairs
/ mz /	homes, tomes, hams, clams, grams, jams, dams, cams, plums, plumes, fumes, blooms, dooms, booms, grooms
/ nz /	vines, lines, whines, signs, vans, tans, plans, vanes, planes, trains, tones, stones, groans, loans, clowns
/ ŋz /	rings, slings, cleanings, tinglings, kings, things, stings, belongings, songs, sarongs, tongs, thongs, wrongs

The plural that consists of a weak-stressed indeterminate vowel, plus a buzz / -iz /, is heard as an inflection after nouns that end in sounds whose articulation makes it physiologically difficult and unnatural for a speaker of English to articulate either a simple hiss or buzz immediately afterward. A vowel sound must intervene. Terminal sounds of this kind may be either voiced or unvoiced: / s / and / z /; / č / and / ǰ /; and / š / and / ž /. Common examples are:

/ siz /	horses, hisses, gases, doses, classes, glasses, spices, losses, houses (where the first s becomes a buzz also)
/ ziz /	buzzes, cheeses, hoses, sizes, glazes, roses, blazes

/ čiz /   clutches, crutches, hutches, hitches, catches, hatches, blotches, churches, niches, switches, swatches, matches

/ jiz /   judges, rages, pages, cages, ages, ridges, images, midges, garages (some speakers)

/ šiz /   wishes, lashes, dashes, rashes, splashes, crashes, flashes, dishes, fishes (often in a Biblical context)

/ žiz /   mirages, loges, doges, garages (some speakers)

In recognizing these sound-spelling relationships, children should be helped to learn first the printed and written forms of words already familiar in speech. After that, pupils should be helped, but only so far as direct experience proves necessary, to make their own generalizations and to apply them to words they have not yet learned to read and write. As a general rule, learners should be helped to develop their own inductive generalizations as a function of the entire process of learning to read and write. The most important learning at this primary level is mastery of the structure and function of known language patterns when they are graphically represented in writing and print.

A discussion of the noun plural inflection / -s / would not be complete without a mention of some of the irregular plurals of our language. We have a number of ways of forming plurals; several sets of nouns do not add / -s / to the base, but form their plurals otherwise: *child, children; ox, oxen; man, men; woman, women; foot, feet; goose, geese; tooth, teeth; mouse, mice.* These form changes are relics of the system of grammatical inflections of Old English, used in the ninth and tenth centuries, A.D.; now largely eroded away in the process of everlasting change in the language. Other systematic irregularities, not inflectional, are due to processes now inactive, like *wife, wives; leaf, leaves; loaf, loaves; life, lives;* etc. Children must learn these forms as exceptions to the general system. Linguistically alert youngsters will make many early mistakes by following their generalizations into language areas that are exceptional (*mans, moneys, cutted, runned, buyed*); such children should be praised for their grasp of the system, for these are the salt of the earth.

Four other common English nouns have two plurals that occur now and then in print: *die, dies* (for coining, shaping, stamping, cutting, or molding); *die, dice* (for many games, including shooting dice); *penny, pence* (British); and *cow, cows, cow, kine* (now archaic, but occasionally found in a poem). Words like *deer, sheep, fish* are the same in both singular and plural forms; but *fishes* may occur, denoting the species of fish, or as an archaism. Without presenting here the several sets of words of foreign origin that take irregular plural forms, because they constitute advanced vocabulary problems rather than primary structural items, we should note finally that children must observe the common rule of changing nouns ending in *-y* to nouns ending in *-ies,* to form the plural (but in sound adding only a buzz / -z /): *baby, babies; cherry, cherries; puppy, puppies; kitty, kitties; guppy, guppies; pony, ponies.* Children understand exceptions if they are explained simply as exceptions, but exceptions having a long and often fascinating history behind them. A child might embark on a career of language scholarship as a result of such a casual explanation by a patient and perceptive parent or teacher.

In their basic reading experience, children still must learn the archaic genitive (or "possessive") inflections, which have dwindled into "the apostrophe *s*" (-'*s*) for singular nouns, and often "the *s* apostrophe" (-*s*') for plural nouns. The apostrophe marking the genitive inflection in English writing is a pest and a nuisance. It corresponds to nothing whatever in speech (where no one misses it), yet it costs good money to print, and receives undue attention in the writing, reading, revision and "correction" of compositions. The genitive inflection itself is a relic from ages past. It is actually a contraction of an ancient inflectional ending, from a time when the structural relationships of words in the mother tongue were largely signaled by a complex system of form changes. It persists, a fossil form in the graphic system of today, and so must be taught, but with a tempering of the wind to the lamb.

The noun inflected with -'s does not pattern at all like the noun with the plural inflection -s. Nouns with -'s fit into the adjective position in the noun groups, as *Bob's mother,* or *the boy's mother.* The -'s of the manual-graphic systems represents about the same sounds as the noun plural -s: *cat, cat's, cats, cats'; dog, dog's, dogs, dogs'; house, house's* / *siz* /, *houses* and *houses'* / *ziz* /. Though there are irregular substitutes for the plural -s, there are none for the genitive -'s. But if a noun already ends in -s—/ -s /, / -z /, or / -iz /—we may simply add the apostrophe in writing, where it is "silent," as in the *the Jones' car;* we may add the -'s, however, as in *the Jones's car,* where the echo of the old inflection is clearer / -iz /. With plurals that end in -s, we add the "silent" apostrophe: *the boys' locker room, the girls' gym.* Irregular plurals take -'s / -z /: *children's books, women's lounge, men's smoker.* Perhaps someday the apostrophe will fade completely from the graphic system of the republic. It has an historical rather than functional excuse for its existence in the genitive inflection (or in contractions). It is a visual myth.

Not only nouns but English verbs also have singular and plural forms determined and signaled by the number of the subject, in the terminology of traditional grammar, though plural as applied to verbs has a different sense. The third person singular subject (N, *he, she,* or *it*) regularly selects a verb with an -s inflection; like the noun plural, it is articulated as / -s /, / -z /, or / -iz /, according to the same phonological principles we discussed earlier in connection with noun plurals. Some familiar examples are:

| / -s / | N, | *he, she,* or *it* | *sits* / -s /. |

| / -z / | N, | *he, she,* or *it* | *stands* / -z /. |

| / -iz / | N, | *he, she,* or *it* | *budges* / -iz /. |

Regular verbs have inflections for the past, spelled -d and -ed, and pronounced / -t /, / -d /, and / -id /, parallel with the sounds of the third person singular inflection. A few examples follow:

/ -t /	The boy	dropped / -t /	the ball.
/ -d /	The girl	learned / -d /	her lesson.
/ -id /	The teacher	regretted / -id /	the error.

Most children know the sound of the verb inflections from several years of preschool experience as chatterboxes. They have to learn spelling and the configurations of words in writing and print.

Compared to verbs in many other languages, the English verb has very few forms, ranging from eight forms of *be* to the single form of *must*, which has dwindled to a marker. Representing verbs with the symbol V, we may illustrate the five structural parts as follows: V for the base form; V-s for the form known in traditional grammar as the third person singular; V-ed for the past; V-ing for the present participle; V-ed/en for the past participle. Although many verbs actually have only three or four, instead of five different parts, or inflectional forms, nearly all verbs can fulfill these five functions by using the same form in more than one function.

To return, for illustration, to the four-part verb *play* from an earlier chapter, we may illustrate the five common functions as follows:

V	V-s	V-ed	V-ing	V-ed/en
play	plays	played	playing	played

The verb *ride* illustrates the five-part verb:

V	V-s	V-ed	V-ing	V-ed/en
ride	rides	rode	riding	ridden

The four verbs *write, drive, smite,* and *rise* are exactly parallel, but the common little verb *bite* differs in the **V-ed** form. Probably not even a precocious child would say, *He* **bote** *his tongue,* though he might say **bited.**

V	V-s	V-ed	V-ing	V-ed/en
bite	bites	bit	biting	bitten

A few common verbs like *set* have only three forms. The base form doubles as **V-ed** and **V-ed/en.**

V	V-s	V-ed	V-ing	V-ed/en
set	sets	set	setting	set

Other verbs that pattern in this way are **bid, burst, cost, cut, hit, hurt, let, shut,** and **spread.**

Some of the four-part verbs change the vowel sound to form **V-ed.** Among these some employ the final consonant sound **/ -t /** and spell both **V-ed** and **V-ed/en** forms with a final *-t:*

V	V-ed
creep	crept
weep	wept

Verbs similar in this patterning include: *feel, felt; sweep, swept; keep, kept.*

Some other four-part verbs change both sound and spelling from *-d* to *-t* to make the **V-ed** and **V-ed/en** forms:

V	V-ed
bend	bent
send	sent
spend	spent

Still other four-part verbs change the vowel and also change the final consonant sounds, usually to / -t / to form **V-ed** and **V-ed/en:**

V	V-ed
bring	brought
catch	caught
seek	sought
teach	taught
think	thought

Make, where the final sound in **V-ed** becomes / -d /, is an exception to the final / -t / change in these verbs.

V	V-ed
make	made

Children should be helped to understand that the sound-spelling differences in verbs are structural in essence and not just matters of individual sounds. And adults should keep in mind that most children know most of the sounds before they enter kindergarten. They also know many verb form changes operationally. That is, children talk.

A number of common verbs in everyday language are composed of a verb-adverb combination where both structure and meaning are so interlinked that the expression amounts to a sort of compound verb; some grammarians refer to this structure as a fused adverb or verb-adverb construction. These verb structures are often composed from a set of familiar verbs like *come, get, give, look, put, hold, draw,* and *pull,* with a set of adverbs that have the same form as prepositions, like *up, over, through, on, in, out,* and the like. Familiar examples are *get up, give up, pull up, draw up, hold back, draw on.* When a noun follows a verb in the **N V N** pattern, the adverb may follow either the verb or the noun, but it must be included in one place or the other to complete the structure: "He *put away* his bat and ball" or "He *put* his bat and ball *away.*" Either pattern is good English and should be included in experience charts and other early reading materials. There is no reason why one should be proscribed; nor should children be told they must "never use a preposition to end a sentence with."

There is one important exception to the flexible distribution of the verb and the adverb in sentences: when a pronoun replaces the second noun function in **N V N** sentences that use the verb-adverb combination in the verb function, the pronoun always comes between the verb and the adverb, never after the adverb. We say, *He put them away,* not *He put away them.* This point troubles some American youngsters and many foreigners of all ages. Other exceptions include pairs that occur with contrasting meanings. For example, *get it on* means to mount a tire, don a garment, replace a mechanical part; while *get on it* might mean to board a train or bus, or in slang, to begin at once on a task. Or *look it over* means to examine, inspect, while *look over it* simply means to lift the eyes above or beyond some object blocking the view.

In Chapter 6 we also mentioned the linguistic principle of contrasting form as a useful teaching device, and illustrated it with contrasting prepositions in phrases of contrasting meanings (page 127). A similar device for language arts instruction, excellent for structural emphasis in reading and writing, is calling the children's attention to families of words having the same base but with word-form changes for each of the four word classes. It is often easier for a child to recognize all the members of an obviously related group or family by association than to accumulate the words as individual vocabulary items—if, when, and as they may happen to occur in his reading. Once he grasps the abstract principle, many a child will associate other words with their families inductively, without specific prompting from parent or teacher.

Following are a few examples of words exhibiting contrast, or objective opposition, in the four classes.

NOUN	VERB	ADJECTIVE	ADVERB
strength	strengthen	strong	strongly
sadness	sadden	sad	sadly
activity	act	active	actively
beauty	beautify	beautiful	beautifully

Examples of this principle should be quietly but helpfully mentioned as they occur in language arts instruction.

Another useful contrast is exhibited in closely related verbs and nouns. The following pairs are illustrative: *sale* and *sell; lose* and *loss; fear* and *fright* (also *fear*); *give* and *gift; breathe* and *breath.*

Especially appealing to children is the contrast of verbs showing attractive actions with nouns ending in *-er* to denote agents who perform the actions. A few common examples are *help* and *helper; work* and *worker; paint* and *painter; swim* and *swimmer; run* and *runner; give* and *giver; teach* and *teacher.* Children in elementary grades can add their own pairs to such a list. Youngsters are just the ones to appreciate the structural riddle, "What is red and green and eats rocks?" A red and green rock-eater, of course.

Still another set of contrasting structural pairs appeals to youngsters and is familiar to them. These are paired nouns and adjectives, where nouns are converted to adjectives by a variety of endings: *nose* and *nosey; dirt* and *dirty; fear* and *fearful* (also *fearsome*); *wood* and *wooden* (also *wooded* and *woody*); *dream* and *dreamy; cream* and *creamy; friend* and *friendly; gold* and *golden; danger* and *dangerous; help* and *helpful; heat* and *hot* (but *cold* and *cold*). Let the children expand such lists at will.

Adjectives and adverbs are word classes partly distinct from each other and partly overlapping. As we saw in our discussion of verbs, adverbs also overlap with some prepositions. (In traditional grammar, adjectives are said to limit or modify nouns, and adverbs to limit or modify verbs or entire sentences.) Many, but not all, adjectives may be compared, as traditional grammar has it: their inflectional forms are *-er* and *-est*, as in *warm, warmer,* and *warmest*. But it is the shorter adjectives, the one-syllable ones, that are most likely to inflect in this way; longer adjectives are usually preceded, instead, by *more* or *most*. Form alone is of less help in differentiating adjectives and adverbs than nouns and verbs, yet in basic reading, attention should be called to these fickle, evasive word-form changes as they occur.

Many adverbs end in *-ly*, like *quickly, hardly, slowly, badly;* but so do some adjectives, like *lovely, manly, womanly, sickly. Hard, fast,* and *slow* are adjectives in *hard man, fast horse,* and *slow time,* but adverbs in *play hard, talk fast,* and *drive slow. Quick* functions as an adjective in *quick look,* and an adverb in *look quick; over* as an adverb in *get over an illness,* a preposition in *get over the fence*. We say *drive slow, drive slowly; look quick, look quickly*.

Remember the couplet from Mother Goose:

Jack be nimble, Jack be quick,
Jack jump over the candlestick.

Jack is asked to be "quick" in the old sense of "lively." This sense of *quick* is related to the *quick* under the fingernail; or to be "hurt to the quick." There is an old saying, recorded in the Bible, where *quick* simply means alive, not dead:

the quick and the dead

These short, familiar words that have to be listed among both the adjectives and the adverbs come down to us from olden times. They are rightly used when they ring true in the ear of a native speaker. In experience charts, and other primary reading-writing instruction, they should be used without question as they come from the lips of the children. It is not helpful to try to purify and correct the children's usage, even when they chance to be "wrong." If they are taught they are "wrong" in their first steps toward literacy, they may never regain enough confidence to be right again.

Certain irregular adjectives and adverbs are common enough and peculiar enough to deserve mention in a book designed for basic reading instruction.

A	Ad	A/Ad -er	A/Ad -est
good		better	best
	well	better	best
bad		worse	worst
	badly	worse	worst
far		farther	farthest
	far	further	furthest
old		elder	eldest
		older	oldest
little	little	less	least

A gentle, incidental method of teaching will prove most effective in conveying these minor but important patterns to elementary school children, always as parts of larger language patterns.

Adjectives are often made up of a noun base plus one of several endings; these endings are a set of word-form changes commonly known as derivational suffixes. Early reading experiences (as well as later) can be clarified and sharpened by incidental but consistent reference to this principle whenever such structures as the following occur in reading and writing:

-able, peaceable	*-al*, accidental	*-an*, European
-ar, polar	*-ary*, honorary	*-ate*, collegiate
-ed, bearded	*-en*, wooden	*-ful*, careful
-ic, angelic, historic	*-ical*, historical	*-ine*, crystalline
-ish, boyish	*-less*, hopeless	*-like*, doglike
-ly, fatherly	*-ous*, famous	*-some*, troublesome
-y, windy		

Likewise, adjectives may be composed of a verb base plus one of several derivational suffixes:

-able, adaptable	*-ible*, reversible	*-ant*, reliant
-al, continual	*-ent*, excellent	*-ful*, forgetful
-ate, considerate	*-ous*, studious	*-ive*, creative
-ory, congratulatory	*-some*, cuddlesome	*-y*, sticky

Similarly, adverbs are often composed of a base from another word class, plus an ending that converts it. For example, many adverbs are composed of an adjective plus *-ly*, as in *badly, gladly;* a noun plus *-ly*, as in *daily, weekly, yearly;* by prefixing *a-* to a noun, as in *asea, abed, afoot;* or by compounding with various endings, as in *sometime, backward, sideways, anywhere, crosswise.* But there are some adverbs that are simple adverbs, such as *fast, hard, here, where, then,* and *thus.* And as we have seen before, some adverbs are exactly the same in form as prepositions; only their distribution in a larger pattern tells us what class or set they belong to in that use.

This observation brings us round once again to the central meaning of this book. A language can only be understood as a structural system capable of generating meaning-bearing patterns; a language cannot be understood as a "vocabulary," a word list, or even as a whole dictionary. Reading is a language-related process that requires taking in, all at once, patterns of structure and meaning well above the level of the word. This applies with special force to learning to read the language we were born to, a vastly different process from learning to read a completely unknown tongue.

If children love Lewis Carroll's poem "Jabberwocky," it is only partly because they feel a kinship with the fay mathematician-poet and his wise-seeming nonsensical doubletalk. It is perhaps even more because of the topsy-turvy linguistic play of the verse. In the following version, elements are italicized that all of us, and the children too, recognize as parts of the structural system of English.

JABBERWOCKY

'*Twas* brillig, *and the* slithy tove*s*
   Did gyre *and* gimble *in the* wabe:
All mims*y were the* borogove*s,*
   And the mome rath*s outgrabe.*

"*Beware the* Jabberwock, *my* son!
   The jaw*s that* bite, *the* claw*s that* catch!
Beware the Jubjub bird, *and* shun
   The frum*ious* Bandersnatch!"

He took *his* vorp*al* sword *in* hand:
   Long time *the* manx*ome* foe *he* sought—
So rest*ed he by the* Tumtum tree,
   And stood awhile *in* thought.

And as in uff*ish* thought *he* stood,
   The Jabberwock, *with* eye*s of* flame,
Came whiffl*ing through the* tulg*ey* wood,
   And burbl*ed as it* came!

One, two! One, two! And through and through
   The vorp*al* blade went snicker-snack!
He left *it* dead, *and with its* head
   He went galumph*ing* back.

"*And hast thou* slain *the* Jabberwock?
   Come *to my* arm*s, my* beam*ish* boy!
O frabj*ous* day! Callooh! Callay!"
   He chortl*ed in his* joy.

'*Twas* brillig, *and the* slithy tove*s*
   Did gyre *and* gimble *in the* wabe:
All mims*y were the* borogove*s,*
   And the mome raths *outgrabe.*

Word analysis, spelling-sound relationships, and similar break-downs should be learned inductively as part of the larger process of associating graphic counterparts of language patterns with their spoken models. The forms of pronouns may be similarly learned; in this book, pronouns are regarded as structure words, or a subset of nouns.

The next chapter presents a further discussion of word analysis, on the level of sounds and spelling, or phonics, and explains what a successful teacher of reading should be conscious of in order to teach reading as a language-related process.

CHAPTER EIGHT

*Spelling,
word analysis,
and phonics*

The letters of our alphabet are arbitrary graphic symbols used by many peoples speaking many languages. They have no sounds, and they make no sounds; when we talk we are not in any sense "pronouncing letters." We articulate basic sound units in closely connected sequences, or series, in which each of these units is modified to some extent by its immediate environment of sound, or by the physiological requirements of articulating any given sequence of sounds. These basic sound units are the *phonemes* of speech. The relationship of the phonemic system to the spelling system is an important consideration in spelling, word analysis, and phonics. Later in this chapter we examine the system of phonemes in detail. An illustrated explanation of the phonemic system in relation to the speech mechanism may be studied in the appendix, "The Human Speech Instrument."

Letters may be arranged so as to form written or printed symbols that graphically represent spoken words, but spoken words are normally integrated into larger structural patterns, heard as intermittent bursts of sound in a rhythmic, melodic stream. It is true that the graphic system does influence the spoken—through education and reading—but altogether, this influence is slight as contrasted to the slow but vast shifting and drifting of sounds, constantly in process in the living tongue, without relation to writing and print.

At least in our language, spelling and the alphabetical principle apply primarily to the actual physical process of *writing,* literally the writing by hand and typing of messages. They apply only secondarily to *reading* the written and printed product. Writing is an active communicative operation, comparable to *speaking:* it is *sending;* reading, on the other hand, is a relatively passive process (but passive in this sense only), comparable to *auding:* it is *receiving.* This broad contrast of the sending and receiving operations of writing and reading may suggest a reason why good spellers are often poor readers, and poor spellers good readers. Whatever the interconnections may be, *spelling is not reading,* and *reading is not spelling.*

English spelling began to be standardized about five hundred years ago, largely owing to the efforts of printers and in association with the spread of printing and printed books. By a perverse coincidence, printing was invented at a time when a number of English dialects had similar but not identical writing systems; distinctive differences of basic sounds, lesser differences of graphic symbols for sounds: confusion was at its height. The development of printers' standard spellings partly mediated and partly maintained the confusion. The truth is, the spelling system at the phonemic level was not very good to begin with, and it has not improved with age; what makes our spelling system work so well—and it does work surprisingly well—is probably the regular spelling of structural word-form changes, and of prefixes and suffixes, *regardless of differences in their sounds*. While spellings have remained essentially the same, the phonemic system has changed greatly since the invention of printing, along with changes in other distinctive and significant features of the language system. For the study of spelling, and of word analysis in that sense, an historical approach would be more enlightening than a phonemic. It would show greater regularity than might immediately strike the eye of a man from Mars. But the historical approach does not seem practicable for teaching children to read and write.

As we have seen in previous chapters, (1) intonation, (2) function order in sentence patterns, (3) structure words, and (4) word-form changes are of greater significance than individual words in American English. These four signaling systems serve in about that order of significance in the language system as a whole. Since words occur in groups within larger structural and meaning-bearing patterns, according to the workings of an intermeshing system, our teaching of reading should stress larger patterns than the single word even when teaching individual words. It remains to be established precisely how much analysis of sound-letter relationships within words is required in reading and in reading instruction, or in composition, for that matter. The patternless reading of many pupils at all levels suggests that we have paid too much attention to the alphabetical principle, and to words singled out of their normal structures. This is one fatal flaw in most phonics methods; another is unsound and false information about sound-spelling relationships.

Because we have all been educated to read and write, and perhaps because we are inundated with printed matter—texts of speeches, for example—we tend to exaggerate the importance of the graphic system, reversing the basic relationship between the primary audio-lingual and the secondary manual-visual symbol systems. "Words" are distinctly separated in writing and print, not in living speech, even carefully articulated and formal speech. Intonation alone accounts for most of the rhythmic grouping and clustering of sounds that characterizes native American speech.

In the sound system of American English, there are between thirty-one and thirty-three "segmental phonemes," depending on regional dialects. Segmental phonemes are the basic consonant and vowel sounds of the language. They are called *segmental* because they were originally thought of as segments or sequential divisions (tiny slices) of the continuous stream of language sounds: they are the distinctive, or significant, basic sound units of speech. The consonant phonemes are fairly stable, but the vowels are shifty between dialects, though relatively stable within any given dialect; speaking technically, the vowels within one dialect do "shift" somewhat according to differences of rate or of stress in larger intonation patterns. Every native speaker who teaches the young idea how to read and write must work out for himself the systematic relationships between standard spellings and the children's regional versions of the sounds they "stand for." While his own dialect should interest him, he has made his own rough adjustment of spelling to his own sounds. The children must learn to relate their sound system to standard spellings, how to write down their familiar sounds in standard spellings, and how to read off their own speech from the printed page.

As a beginning, a look at a phonemic alphabet may be helpful. In such an alphabet, the pure alphabetical principle is rigorously applied: each basic sound-signal is represented by one graphic symbol and one only. There are no digraphs or trigraphs as in English spelling, and no symbol represents one phoneme in this instance and another in that. One sound: one symbol; and the starting point is always speech, a variety of spoken English as represented by one or several native users of it.

The phonemic system described here is generally Midwestern; specifically of that northern section including Michigan, Minnesota, and Northern Illinois, where the author has spent most of his life; more specifically, it is that of one speaker, his family, and those among his colleagues, advisers, and friends who are native to the region. Readers should not quarrel with details of the presentation, but simply modify it as their two good ears tell them to in order to represent the speech of their particular region. There is no one single correct way to produce or notate the sounds of our language, except that phonemic notation of speech is "correct" if it exactly represents the sounds actually made.

As a graphic device of linguistic notation, a pair of virgules, or slant lines / / enclosing phonemic symbols, is used to signify that the symbols are not letters but representations of *sound units*. (Phonetic notation uses brackets: [ ].) We need this frame because many of the letters of our alphabet are used also as phonemic symbols, with a few new symbols introduced in order to represent all the phonemes. For example, $/p/$ means the phoneme represented by that symbol, not the letter *p*. The letter *p* often represents nothing but silence, as in *pneumonia* or *psychology;* yet often $/p/$ occurs without an equivalent visual symbol in the graphic system: after *warm* in the word *warmth,* for instance, where the physiological requirements of rapid and easy articulation of English demand the $/p/$ for transition between two consonant sounds that cannot be uttered naturally in that sequence. **Warm** plus *th* is required by a structural feature of the language system (compare wid*th,* leng*th,* bread*th*); $/p/$ is needed to get from $/m/$ to $/\theta/$ (*th*). The $/k/$ before *-th* in *length* is a parallel instance. (How many times has a child been "corrected" by a mistaken teacher for "pronouncing a letter that is not there" in *warmth* or *length?*)

The phoneme may be defined as the smallest significant class of speech sounds. In this definition the terms *significant* and *class* deserve special note. *Significant* means that the sound makes a distinctive difference in the language system; it is unique, different from all other phonemes in the system. Native speakers attend to it in its uniqueness; the brain, sorting spoken sounds like a computer, groups them into phonemes, according to whether or not they are distinctive and significant in the given system—or ignores them. Slight variations of the sound (which another language might use as signals) are ignored as nonsignificant; these variations, called *allophones,* comprise each particular significant *class* of sounds, or the phoneme. For example, four allophones of $/p/$ occur in the series: *pet, spot, suppose, top;* they are phonetically slightly different, but phonemically identical. Here is the essential difference between phonemic and phonetic analysis: phonemic analysis, simpler and more functional than phonetic, deals only with sounds significant in the language system and ignores nonsignificant differences.

In listing the consonant phonemes, the useful and significant contrast of "voiced" and "voiceless" pairs is presented below. Many native speakers are amazed to learn that when they speak, they produce voiceless sounds when they are not whispering. (In a whisper, we substitute friction for voicing.) Actually, the segmented stream of speech includes (1) voiced speech sounds, (2) voiceless speech sounds, and (3) the normal soundless intervals and interruptions of the speech flow which follow junctures and terminals. Contrasting pairs of consonant phonemes are arranged here in words illustrating the initial position where feasible. So far as possible, they are listed in words that use the six most common simple vowels, arranged in order. Practice reading them aloud, clearly and distinctly.

Voiceless $/p/$ and voiced $/b/$
Voiceless $/p/$ — *pat, pet, pit, pot, putt, put*
Voiced $\quad/b/$ — *bat, bet, bit, bottle, but, book*

Voiceless $/t/$ and voiced $/d/$
Voiceless $/t/$ — *tap, ten, tip, tot, tub, took*
Voiced $\quad/d/$ — *dad, den, dip, dot, duck*

Voiceless $/k/$ and voiced $/g/$

Voiceless / k / — cap, ken, kit, cot, cut, could
Voiced / g / — gap, get, gift, got, gun, good

Voiceless / s / and voiced / z /
Voiceless / s / — sat, set, sit, sock, sup, stood
Voiced / z / — has, Zen, zip, nozzle, puzzle

Voiceless / f / and voiced / v /
Voiceless / f / — fat, fettle, fit, father, funny, foot
Voiced / v / — vat, vessel, vintage, volcano, vulture

Voiceless / θ / and voiced / ð /
Voiceless / θ / — lath, Seth, thin, thunder
Voiced / ð / — than, then, this, bother, thus

Voiceless / š / and voiced / ž /
Voiceless / š / — shad, shed, ship, shot, shut, shook
Voiced / ž / — azure, leisure, vision (/ ž / does not occur
initially in English except in the exotic
names Zha Zha and Gigi)

Voiceless / č / and voiced / ǰ /
Voiceless / č / — chap, check, chip, chop, chuck
Voiced / ǰ / — jab, gentle, gym, job, jug

This is a visual display of the eight pairs of voiced and voiceless consonants in initial positions, and in words using the six
simple vowels so far as possible. A few differences in spelling
appear unavoidably; variations in spelling will be shown more
systematically later in this discussion.

For the "nasal" continuant consonants, / m / and / n /, and
the "liquids," / l / and / r /, we use phonemic symbols identical
with the letters that commonly represent them in writing and
print. The nasal / ŋ / is commonly spelled ng (sing) but sometimes n (sink).

/ m /   man, men, mid, model, muddle

/ n /   nag, net, nip, knock, nub

/ ŋ /   bang, length, sing, sung (/ ŋ / is never an initial sound
          in English)

/ r /   rag, red, rip, rock, rut, root

/ l /   lap, lens, lit, lock, lump, look

The semivowels, / h /, / w /, and / y /, are usually represented by letters in writing and print when they occur initially. The phonemic symbols are identical with the letters of the alphabet that often (but not always) represent them in the graphic system.

/ h /   had, head, hid, hod, huddle, hood

/ w /   Wac, wet, wit, wad, was, wood

/ y /   yap, yet, yip, yacht, yup

Semivowel phonemes also occur in various combinations following the simple vowels to form the long vowels of English, which are presented later in the discussion, after the simple vowels.

Six simple vowels are very common in American English, / æ /, / e /, / i /, / a /, / ə / (schwa sound), and / u /; a seventh, / ɔ /, is also heard in such words as *caught, nought, bought.* The / o / seldom occurs alone; normally it precedes a semivowel, and the two in sequence make a complex vowel nucleus (long vowel or diphthong). The phonemes / ə / (schwa sound) and / i / (barred *i*) are distributed throughout the language in weak-stressed syllables; they are sometimes described as indeterminate vowel sounds, probably because, in their weak-stressed positions, they are distinguished less sharply from each other and from other vowels than the other simple vowels in syllables receiving greater stress. Following is a presentation of the simple vowel phonemes in word pairs illustrating at the same time the contrasting voiceless and voiced consonant pairs:

/ æ /   *pat, bat; tap, dad; cap, gap; sat, has; fat, vat; thank, than; chap, jab.*

/ e /   *pet, bet; ten, den; ken, get; set, Zen; fettle, vessel; Seth, then; shed, leisure; check, gentle.*

/ i /   *pit, bit; tip, dip; kit, gift; sit, zip; fit, vintage; thin, this; ship, vision; chip, gym.*

/ a /   *pot, bottle; tot, dot; cot, got; sock, nozzle; chop, job.*

/ ə /   *putt, but; tub, duck; cut, gun; sup, puzzle; thunder, thus; chuck, jug;* in weak-stressed syllables: sof*a,* *a*bout, *a*ffect, *e*ffect, below, etc.

/ u /   *put, book; could, good.*

/ ɔ /   *bought, caught, naught, astronaut, taught.*

/ ɨ /   affect, effect, degrade, determine, below, beneath, etc.

/ ə / and / ɨ / appear to be interchangeable in weak-stressed syllables, even in the speech of the same speaker, depending on the phonemic and articulatory environments.

/ o /   the first sound in the "long vowel" / ow /, as in *go;* rarely heard alone.
        poet, boat; tote, dote; coat, goat.

The so-called long and short vowels are traditional but not descriptive names for vowel sounds that are often spelled with the same letters, but are not phonemically related to each other. Long vowel sounds are among the "complex vowel nuclei" of linguistic description; in articulatory terms, they are really smooth, quick movements within one syllable, from a simple vowel position to a semivowel position. The two phonemes are so inextricably interwoven in this process that it is virtually impossible to know where one leaves off and the other begins. The untrained native ear hears the combined phonemes as one vowel sound. The tabulation below contrasts the common long and short vowel sounds in terms of (1) traditional diacritical markings, (2) spellings, and (3) phonemic transcriptions of words in which they occur.

LONG	SHORT
ā as in *fate* / *feyt* /	ă as in *cat* / *kæt* /
ē as in *cede* / *siyd* /	ĕ as in *bed* / *bed* /
ī as in *nine* / *nayn* /	ĭ as in *sit* / *sit* /
ō as in *go* / *gow* /	ŏ as in *hot* / *hat* /
ū as in *cute* / *kyuwt* /	ŭ as in *but* / *bət* /
ū as in *institution, pollution, solution,* etc. / *uw* /	
ōō as in *room* / *ruwm* /	ŏŏ as in *book* / *buk* /

Two of the complex vowel nuclei are diphthongs of traditional terminology; they are usually represented by spelling with two letters: *ou* and *ow* as in *foul* and *fowl* / *fawl* /; and *oy* and *oi*, as in *boy* / *boy* / and *boil* / *boyl* /. Other common words that exhibit the same sounds and spellings are, for / *aw* /: *about, cowl, doubt, growl, house, howl, mouse, joust, roust;* and for / *oy* /: *coin, coil, deploy, employ, foil, join, loin, moil, quoit.*

The selected information presented here is designed as an essential minimum required to understand the phonemic system of American English. But the phonemic system is not the spelling system; as we have noted, the spelling of our words relates to an earlier dialect than our own, dating back about five hundred years, a dialect from far away and long ago. Our spelling contains many relics of forgotten pronunciations. Besides, our spelling system relates more closely to words spoken in isolation than to the familiar sounds of running speech. When we pronounce a word by itself, we give it a heavy, single-word stress rather than the stress it carries in the intonation patterns of the larger structures in which it normally functions; and we tend to exaggerate each individual phoneme somewhat, to the point where the word sounds artificial, unlike itself in real life. We consciously and deliberately pronounce the isolated word as we think it "ought" to be pronounced, often saying it syllable by syllable.

Possibly a little of such practice is necessary, but certainly not drill. If children carry such self-conscious and unnatural articulation over into their reading, either oral or silent, they are likely to proceed word by word, so as to produce a dull, broken patterning, foreign to the easy rhythmic and melodic flow of native speech. In word-by-word reading, every word is as good as every other word, just as it is in a dictionary, or a vocabulary list, with no differentiation of intonation and function. *This is not true reading.* Whatever attention to word analysis and spelling may be needed in reading instruction, isolated words should always be brought back into the larger patterns and structures that function linguistically and carry meaning: *this is true reading.*

No clear correlation exists between spelling ability and reading ability; as noted before, a good reader may be a poor speller, and a poor reader may be a good speller. It seems likely, however, that a good reader will accurately pick up word-form changes, prefixes, suffixes, and other regularly spelled clues to meaning-bearing structural patterns that are represented graphically on the printed page. Otherwise he cannot be a good reader.

Even in writing and composition, spelling may be of minor importance in primary instruction. Professor Ivah Green, writing in *Elementary English,* gives a visiting teacher's impression of the work of first graders who were encouraged to go ahead and write whatever they wanted to say, regardless of spelling, punctuation, and the niceties of composition. Here are four examples of the uncorrected writing of six-year-olds, from "All Words Belong to First Graders."[1]

MY DOLLY

My dolly is buerock. Her lag came off. My brother buerockn it. I am not happy now.

A LITTLE GIRL

Once a ponn a time there was a little girl. She was just old unof too go to school. When she startoed of too school she wonedered where her dog was. And she looked and looked. But she just couldont find her dog. So she went to school. And he was follene her to school.

SPERYING

Pretty soon Sperying is coming. Flowres will blom. I will have flowres in are yrard. I will pic them. I will pic red oens and yellow oens and white oens and blue oens to. My mother will pot them in a vays.

MY DANSING DRES

I have a dansing dres. You shod see it wen I twrl. It twrls way owt. I can dans in it. I can stan on my toes too.

The visiting teacher comments:

1. Those children *wanted* to write.

2. They wanted to write about what was on their minds most at that particular moment.

3. They were not frustrated in their expression by inability to spell big words, or unusual ones. So they spelt them the way they thought they sounded. Their teacher would tell them the correct way, later. They would add these words to their word lists to be used in telling a story.

4. Pupils were aware that words were to be used in telling a story.

5. Anything they wanted to tell their teacher and classmates in written form was acceptable.

6. *Pupils knew how to put punctuation in their voices as they read their stories aloud,* even if they sometimes forgot to put periods on the blackboard or paper [emphasis added].

7. Pupils were learning that sometimes words were spelled just as they sounded; at other times they were spelled differently. They would learn how to do them all right in time.

Although the visiting teacher indicated no explicit linguistic orientation, her insights are those of an attentive listener and warm human being. The spirit of her insights into basic teaching of the mother tongue shows implicit linguistic grasp, reminiscent of the earlier work of Grace M. Fernald. Fernald recommended, however, that *children's original stories should be correctly type-written for them to use as a basis for both reading and writing.*[2]

Reading and writing may be thought of, figuratively, as mirror images of each other, different but corresponding sides of the manual-graphic system of representing the language. As Professor Green suggests in the article cited above, it is entirely possible that spelling might best be learned inductively in the primary grades, in relation to mastering the larger patterns. If it were not in fact learned by that method, however, then would be the time to treat it more systematically (if we parents and educators can learn how). In any case, the person teaching the language arts must himself have mastered spelling in order to teach it. Some minimum of correct spelling, so far undetermined, is probably needed for successful reading in the higher grades and in later life. (The sociopsychological shibboleth character of "correct" spelling is omitted from this discussion, because it is unrelated to specific linguistic functions.)

Division of words into syllables is primarily a printer's device rather than a problem of reading or writing; words should seldom be artificially uttered as if the syllables were actually separated in speech. *In speech, a syllable is a part of a word containing a vowel and receiving some degree of stress;* a syllable is not a structural element except insofar as it is a part of the characteristic pitch-stress pattern conforming to its functioning in larger structures. Syllables in speech and syllables in print are not the same; on the contrary, they should be clearly differentiated. Mischief has been done in reading instruction by attempting to make children "pronounce all the letters and all the syllables in each word." This stricture applies with special force to so-called "double consonants," as in *letter, butter, ladder, manner, mammoth,* and so on.

Children have been forced to memorize atrocities like "Betty Botter," where the hardest trick (because the most un-English) is to produce two / t / sounds separated by an open juncture for every "double *t.*" Memorization of the following doggerel was required by a seventh-grade teacher as an example and reminder of "correct pronunciation."

Bet/ + /ty Bot/ + /ter

Bet/ + /ty Bot/ + /ter bought some but/ + /ter.

But, she said, this but/ + /ter's bit/ + /ter.

If I put it in my bat/ + /ter,

It will make my bat/ + /ter bit/ + /ter.

But if I buy some bet/ + /ter but/ + /ter,

It will make my bat/+/ter bet/+/ter.

So Bet/+/ty bought some bet/+/ter but/+/ter,

And it made her bat/+/ter bet/+/ter.

This is more than a mnemonic device. It is demonic. Of course these "double consonants" are not double *sounds* at all, but spelling devices for single sounds; linguists call such purely graphic devices for spelling *graphemes*.

In spelling, double consonants usually indicate that the preceding vowel sound is simple, or short, whereas a single consonant for the same sound, when followed by the letter *e*, usually indicates that the preceding vowel sound is a complex vowel nucleus, or long.

Simple vowels (short vowels) Preceding double consonants		Complex vowel nuclei (long vowels) Preceding single consonants followed by letter e		
/æ/	lătter	lāte	/ey/	lāter
/i/	bĭtter	bīte	/ay/	bīter
/ə/	cŭtter	cūte	/yuw/	cūter
/a/	tŏtter	tōte	/ow/	tōter
/e/	bĕtter	mēte	/iy/	mēter

But this is the kind of generalization a child should make for himself inductively, and with a minimum of help from teachers, in the course of learning to read and write. It is very doubtful that he can learn the manual-graphic system by applying such rules deductively, by precept.

We have seen how the consonant phonemes, the simple (short) vowel phonemes, and the vowel nuclei (long vowels) are spelled in a number of common words. Now let us consider *graphemes* that we use to represent the vowel phonemes and the complex vowel nuclei. We need the term *digraph* for those graphemes that use two letters and the term *trigraph* for those that use three letters to represent single vowel or consonant sounds, or complex vowel nuclei. A pure vowel digraph, or simple vowel digraph, is made up of two letters. Examples are: *ea* / *e* / in *bread; ea* / *a* / in *heart; ou* / *u* / in *could; ou* / *ə* / in *double; ou* / *ɔ* / in *cough; oo* / *ə* / in *flood; oo* / *u* / in *foot; oe* / *ə* / in *does; ai* / *æ* / in *plaid; ai* / *e* / in *said; ie* / *e* / in *friend; ei* / *e* / in *heifer*. There is no room here (or anywhere else) for that nonsensical "rule" of phonics:

When two vowels go a-walking,
The first one does the talking.

Consonant digraphs are two-letter graphemes for single consonant sounds: *ch* / *č* / in *church, reach; sh* / *š* / in *ship, rush; ph* / *f* / in *phoneme; dg* / *ǰ* / in *judge, ridge; gh* / *f* / in *cough; gh* / *p* / in *hiccough; ng* / *ŋ* / in *bang, sing, long; wh* / *h* / in *who, whose, whom; th* / *θ* / in *thin, think; th* / *ð* / in *then, these*.

Trigraphs are three-letter graphemes for single consonant or long vowel sounds. A few examples of consonant trigraphs are *chm* in *drachm, tch* in *catch, ght* in *thought*. Long vowel trigraphs include *eye* / *ay* / in *eye; igh* / *ay* / in *sigh; eau* / *ow* / in *beau; uoy* / *oy* / in *buoy*. Beyond these, we have "tetragraph" (four-letter) curiosities as *ough* / *aw* / in *plough* and *phth* / *t* / in *phthisis*.

There are a number of digraphs for the long vowels; you will recall that many of these are the diphthongs of traditional terminology. Linguists call them complex vowel nuclei, because phonemically they are articulated as rapid movements in one syllable from one of the simple vowel positions to one of the semivowel positions.

/ *iy* /   long vowel sound marked $\bar{e}$:

ae in **Caesar**	*ee* in **reed**	*ei* in **receive**
ea in **bead**	*ey* in **key**	*eo* in **people**
ie in **believe**	*ay* in **quay**	*oe* in **amoeba**

/ *ey* /   long vowel sound marked $\bar{a}$:

ea in **great**	*ai* in **rain**	*ay* in **play**
au in **gauge**	*ei* in **rein**	*ao* in **gaol**

/ *ay* /   long vowel sound marked $\bar{\imath}$:

ai in **aisle**	*ie* in **lie**	*ei* in **stein**
uy in **buy**		

/ *ow* /   long vowel sound marked $\bar{o}$:

oa in **oak**	*ow* in **slow**	*ou* in **soul**
ew in **sew**	*oo* in **brooch**	*eo* in **yeoman**
oe in **sloe**		

/ *uw* /   long vowel sound marked $\bar{u}$:

oo in **moon**	*eu* in **neuter**	*ou* in **soup**
oe in **canoe**	*ew* in **news**	

/ *oy* /   traditional diphthongs, oi and oy:

oi in **boil**	*oy* in **boy**

/ *aw* /   traditional diphthongs, ou and ow:

ou in **house**	*ow* in **fowl**

Linguists use the term consonant *cluster* for the term *blend* that is found in many phonics systems; *cluster* seems more accurate because it suggests distinctly heard sequences of consonant phonemes with no intervening vowels. Common consonant clusters are:

bl in *blend*	*br* in *bread*	*cl* in *clock*	*cr* in *crumb*
dr in *drum*	*fl* in *floor*	*fr* in *fresh*	*gl* in *glass*
gr in *grass*	*wh* / *hw* / in *when, where, what, why*, etc. (for some speakers; others have / *w* /)		

qu / *kw* / in *queen*		*sc* in *scout*	*sl* in *sling*
st in *sting*	*pl* in *plum*	*pr* in *print*	*tr* in *train*

rd in *card*	*rk* in *ark*	*rl* in *girl*	*rm* in *arm*
rn in *horn*	*rt* in *start*		

No discussion of sound-spelling relationships in basic reading instruction would be complete without mention of the letters that appear quite commonly but represent no sound whatever in modern English. These have long been known as "silent" letters, not only because they do not represent speech sounds any longer, but because it is thought that the other letters on the printed page *do* represent definite individual sounds, and that we pronounce letters and printed words when we read aloud. We have seen how misleading such an orientation can be, yet all of us have to work at it a bit to keep clear in our minds that writing and print are *secondary* graphic systems based on primary language. Following are letters that often stand "silent" in simple words:

b in *bomb, debt, doubt, dumb, tomb, plumb, thumb*

g in *sign, align, malign, benign, reign*

h in *honor, honest, hour*

k in *know, knowledge, knee, knuckle, knight, knife, knob*

l in *calm, could, would, palm, psalm* (in some dialects, *help*)

n in *autumn, column, hymn* (but note *autumnal, columnar, hymnal*)

p in *psalm, psychology, pneumonia, ptomaine, Ptolemy*

e as a final letter is "silent," but in the spelling system indicates a preceding complex vowel nucleus (long vowel) in one-syllable words such as *ice, ace, home.* (See display on page 178.)

The sort of thing just presented is what impelled the late George Bernard Shaw to assert that in English, the word *fish* might just as well be spelled *ghoti* (and to leave substantial funds in his will to help promote a vast spelling reform). In *ghoti,* if we "sound" *gh* as in *enough, o* as in *women,* and *ti* as in *nation*—true enough, we get *fish* / *fiš* /. But in spelling practice, not a one of the three phonemes is regularly represented in these positions by these graphemes. The *gh* is never used initially; *ti* representing / *š* / does not occur finally but medially—the initial part of a suffix such as *-tion* or *-tiate;* and *o* as / *i* / occurs precisely once in English, in the word *women.* G. B. S. was spoofing again.

To carry the *ghoti* trick to the point of the ridiculous, we may pretend to spell the word *circus p-s-o-l-o-q-u-o-i-s-e* as follows:

circus	/ sərkəs /	psoloquoise
c	/ s /	ps in *psycho*
ir	/ ər /	olo in *colonel*
c	/ k /	qu in *claque*
us	/ əs /	oise in *porpoise*

The game of far-out spellings seems to have gone about as far out
as it can go with the spelling of *potato* as *g - h - e - a - u - p - h - t - h -
e - i - g - h - p - t - o - u - g - h -* :

potato	/ powteytow /	gheauphtheighptough
p	/ p /	gh in *hiccough*
o	/ ow /	eau in *beau*
t	/ t /	phth in *phthisic*
a	/ ey /	eigh in *eight*
t	/ t /	pt in *ptomaine*
o	/ ow /	ough in *though*

Our discussion of strange, irregular spellings would not be
complete without listing the notorious seven groups of phonemes
"spelled" *ough,* some of them cited above. Three are complex
vowel nuclei represented by the words *bough* / aw /, *dough*
/ ow /, and *through* / uw /; four more groups include vowels
terminated by consonants, represented by the words *cough*
/ ɔf /, *enough* / əf /, *hiccough* / əp /, and *lough* / ak /. In
addition, there are two different sets of phonemes "spelled" *ought*
in the words *drought* / awθ / and *thought* / ɔt /.

Spelling and reading are not the same thing at all, but two
quite different processes; the relationship of spelling to reading,
and more especially to basic reading instruction, is not clear, at
least not at the phonemic level. Alphabet and word methods of
instruction (phonics and sight words) *both* tend toward word-by-
word reading, or reading by pattern fragments. Children have

learned to read by all known methods, as well as virtually by themselves; what we need is a methodology that will produce the fewest reading cripples. Despite the irregular and inconsistent relationships we have noted between phonemes and graphemes, an exhaustive listing would show that there are families and groups of words where the correspondences between sounds and spellings are fairly regular. Moreover, as noted earlier, word-form changes, prefixes, suffixes, and other systematic clues to language structure are generally spelled quite regularly without regard to differences in sound; this regularity corresponding to important structural signals probably compensates for irregular spellings at the phonemic level. Persons who are successful in mastering the manual-graphic system no doubt learn most easily to write and to read those language patterns, including individual words, that they actually need at any given point in their development of these skills; on these experiences and observations they base their own inductive generalizations.

At any rate, this is the way we learn to talk.

In mastering speaking and auding, we first learn the gross, general features of the sound system; then as we refine and perfect our control of speech patterns, we make many mistakes, encounter the exceptions piecemeal, and gradually fit the peculiarities in with the regularities so that we achieve (rather early) a native command of the mother tongue. As a scholar-teacher specializing in teaching American English as a native language, orienting my observations in the light of linguistics, I have concluded that learning the graphic system should proceed by analogy to the prior learning of the spoken language. In such an approach to primary manual-visual skills, spelling is not neglected nor ignored, but taken up inductively, and only as needed, until the children have a firm grasp of larger graphic patterns. Formal, deductive spelling instruction at the phonemic level may be introduced in middle and upper grades if the need exists then. Language instruction should be functional at all depths and at all levels of learning.

CHAPTER NINE

*The import
of language
and of reading*

We have completed our walking tour through the structural system of modern American English, with stopovers to pay special attention to basic reading processes. We have surveyed and laid out the tract in large and to some degree in small. It is a rich and various domain. Now is the time to range beyond the closely held limits of our exploration so far, projecting some far-searching questions. Some are age-old queries, some new; all stretch the boundaries of our small map of language and of reading. They enlarge the world.

What is the import of language and of reading? What do we know of the origin of language? How is it possible for man to talk? Does man have special "speech organs"? What can be said about the "languages" of birds and animals? Is it language that makes man man? How many languages are spoken by the races of mankind? How are they related? How did English develop? Is English like Latin? What are the connections of language with conceptual and reflective thought, with human creativity, with imaginative literature? How do these matters relate to reading and writing? What are the ultimate values of literacy?

What attribute, more than any other, distinguishes man from beast?

It is chiefly language that characterizes man as man, language that undergirds and binds together human society and culture, language that unites inner man and outer reality, making for sanity and order. Language is at once the basis and the matrix of man's ability to conceive and execute; it is the medium of his reflective and conceptual thought.

Language and thought are intimately connected from infancy onward, whether we are thinking of the growth of an individual human being, or of the development of the entire human race. Indeed, man's creation of language may be responsible in large part for the evolution of that uniquely complex nervous structure, the human brain.

187   *The import of language and of reading*

All distinctively human activities depend on communication, interaction, and cooperation: between man and man, between culture and culture, between generation and generation. And while man has other and related means of communication, social interaction is essentially and basically linguistic. Man alone has language. Language is man's greatest invention; no other creature shares it with him. Language means literally the use of the tongue in speech. This is language. From language man derives writing and print, graphic representations of language, probably his second greatest invention. In any event auding and speaking develop first, reading and writing much later—whether we are thinking of an individual human life from infancy onward, or the life of the race from the beginning of time.

Language, then, distinguishes man from beast. Language provides the basis of interaction and the means of communication in nearly all subjects and studies, including literature and the arts. None of these is conceivable outside societies and cultures of men who talk.

> Language is not an abstract construction of the learned, or of dictionary-makers, but is something arising out of the work, needs, ties, joys, affections, tastes, of long generations of humanity, and has its bases broad and low, close to the ground.[1]

All races of man have language, all use the same physiological equipment to produce the sounds of language. Yet strictly speaking we have no speech organs as such. That is, all the organs used in speaking had other and more basic functions before they were used to develop the complex cultural phenomenon of language. If we consider these organs as "speech organs," they have much in common with the parts of a musical wind instrument.

Our breathing system contains and controls the pulsating stream of air that emerges from the lips, modulated, overtoned, rhythmed, segmented, and patterned: in a word, language. The deepest inner part of this system is the diaphragm, a powerful layer of muscle and tendons separating the chest from the abdomen; largely involuntary, the movements of the diaphragm can be controlled to perform as a sort of bellows in speech, but speech must conform to the necessities of breath. Above the diaphragm, the lungs, the trachea, and the bronchial tubes provide part of the characteristic resonance of the individual voice. The larynx (Adam's apple) encloses the vocal folds (cords) that open and close the entrance into the trachea (Sunday throat, or windpipe); in speech these vibrating vocal folds produce the air waves that we hear as the sound of the human voice.

When man speaks, the larynx, the pharynx, the mouth and nose cavities, the tongue, lips, and teeth all act in concert to produce the phonation and articulation of sounds. Every normal child has these organs, must develop them, and must learn to use them in their primary physiological functions before turning them to their cultural function—language. The child who has not mastered sucking, swallowing, biting, and chewing will not be able to control the consonant and vowel sounds of language. Most children the world over babble and chatter their language long before they reach school age.

Thousands of languages are currently spoken in the world. Many, like English, have been scientifically studied, and traced far back in recorded history. A great body of significant linguistic knowledge has been accumulated, especially during the present century. But the origin of language is among the unsolved puzzles surrounding the beginnings of man himself. It seems almost certain that we shall never fathom some of these mysteries because, ironically, the nature of the problem excludes either written records or oral tradition going back to the occurrences we seek definite knowledge of. It does seem fairly certain that wherever and whenever early man developed conceptual knowledge that could be communicated—how to make a hunting arrow, for example—language apparently existed. From the earliest times, language and human thought seem always to have been intimately connected.

Even though we shall probably never be able to trace our way clear back to the remotest beginnings of language, rational speculation may be worthwhile because it can strengthen our grasp of the nature of language—and therefore of man. There is intrinsic interest in the curious theories evolved by scholars and philosophers in earlier times. Noah Webster, in the preface to his *American Dictionary*, declared: "Language, as well as the faculty of speech, was the immediate gift of God."[2] This view agrees with the general picture presented in the Old Testament: Adam understood the Lord's words, and named the birds and beasts and all living creatures; Eve conversed with the serpent (rather Satan in the serpent, since man alone could speak). For centuries after the flood, men spoke one language ("The whole earth was of one language, and of one speech"), until the Tower of Babel was built, and cursed men went their multilingual ways.

Medieval theologians debated whether language was the creation of God or man. In the eighteenth century Rousseau portrayed man as assigning certain meanings to certain sounds as part of the social contract, and Herder reasoned that it must have been man who made language, since it had so many weaknesses incompatible with the perfect nature of God. Man's superior intellect, he argued, enabled him to invent language. The beasts remained speechless.

In the nineteenth century a number of ingenious guesses were made, among them the following:

1. The theory of onomatopoeia, or of language imitating the natural sounds of the world, in such words as *bang, crash, splash, purr, sizzle, squeak*

2. Darwin's suggestion that sounds of physiological origin evolved into the interjections of speech

3. The theory that men developed language through cooperative work chants

4. Max Muller's theory that speech somehow "rang" in harmony with the nature of things named by the appropriate sounds

5. F. N. Scott's theory that breathing produced sounds that later acquired meaning (1907)

Also in the twentieth century the great Danish grammarian Jespersen suggested that mankind's early chatter, or song, became conventionalized as communication symbols, or speech; a concept that brought language theory to the verge of modern linguistics and the behavioral sciences.

Parrots and other talking birds merely "parrot" human speech; they do not understand or properly use it. Any talking bird can be taught to say, "Birds don't talk." But what of the "language" of the dog, horse, monkey, ape, or wolf, or of such birds as wild ducks and crows? Many creatures communicate by vocal and other signs, yet they do not have language. What is the difference?

Speculating on the basis of the guesses and theories of earlier psychologists and linguists, the French psychologist, Joseph Vendryes, said that the difference between the language of animals and of men is that man's language is symbolic.[3] "Psychologically the original linguistic act consists in giving to a sign a symbolic value. This psychological process distinguishes the language of man from that of animals."[4] Thus, a dog may warn by barking when a stranger approaches, an adult partridge may cluck to its chicks to take cover; but neither can make any practical use of such signs except in the presence of danger, as a direct warning of it. Beasts and birds cannot use their signs as symbols, independently of the thing indicated, the referent. Man can. Language makes man man.

Man's language is a code or system of spoken symbols, his greatest invention; graphic symbols comprise a derivative, or secondary system, his second greatest invention. Writing and printing are the manual-visual employment of a graphic code that represents, but only partially, the audio-lingual code of language itself. Since the spoken code symbolically represents human experience and outer reality, graphic language processes (reading-writing) deal with a double system of linguistic symbols, the graphic derived from the spoken.

Of the two hundred or so families of languages in the world, the Indo-European family is best known to Western scholars. American English belongs to this great family of tongues. Scholars agree that a parent language, proto-Indo-European, originated before the dawn of writing, and was spoken by a people who lived east of the Baltic Sea and north of the Crimean. Through migration, settlement and intermarriage, this people established communities and nations north and west to the Atlantic Ocean, south to the Mediterranean Sea, and southeast as far as India.

Eventually the various groups developed their own distinctive languages, so that descendants speaking various derived tongues cannot understand each other without study. Scholars generally divide Indo-European into Indo-Iranian, Balto-Slavic, Hellenic, Italic, Celtic, Armenian, Albanian, and Germanic. Our language— American English—belongs to the Germanic group. It is quite distinct from Latin and all its modern descendants, French, Spanish, Portuguese, Italian, and Rumanian. But neither the Germanic, from which English derives its structure, nor the Italic group, from which English derives about one-fourth of its words, explains our language: the best approach to American English is through study of American English itself. Though basic linguistic principles are at work in all languages, each is best studied in its own terms.

Traditionally, the history of the English language is divided, somewhat arbitrarily, into three major periods:

1. Old English, or Anglo-Saxon, from the earliest beginnings to about 1100
2. Middle English, from 1100 to 1500
3. Modern English, from 1500 to today

Modern English may be further divided into Early Modern English, 1500 to 1700, and Late Modern, since 1700. Viewed more broadly, the English language has passed through continental and island periods of development, and is now increasingly a global language.

Without going into a detailed analysis, we may derive some instruction simply from looking at the Lord's Prayer in the familiar King James translation (1611) and comparing it with an Old English version of a thousand years ago.

| *Our Father* | *which art in heaven,* | *Hallowed be thy name.* |
| **Faeder ure** | **ðu ðe eart on heofonum** | **si ðin nama gehalgod.** |

| *Thy kingdom come.* | *Thy will be done* |
| **To becume in rice.** | **Gewurðe in willa** |

in earth   as it is in heaven.
on earðan   swa swa on heofonum.

Give us this day   our daily bread.
Urne gedaeghwamlican hlaf   syle us to daeg.

And forgive us our debts,   as we forgive our debtors.
**And forgyf us ure gyltas   swa swa we forgyfa urum
                                gyltendum.**

And lead us not into temptation,
And ne gelaed ðu us on costnunge

but deliver us from evil.   Amen.
ac alys us of yfele.   Soðlice.

Now compare the Old English and the King James versions
of the Lord's Prayer with a Latin rendering.

**Pater, noster, qui es in coelis, sanctificetur nomen tuum;
adveniat regnum tuum: fiat voluntas tua, sicut in coelo, et in
terra. Panem nostrum quotidianum da nobis hodie, et dimitte
nobis debita nostra, sicut et nos dimittimus debitoribus nostris.
Et ne nos inducas in tentationem: sed libera nos a malo. Amen.**

Structurally the Latin bears little resemblance to the English.
Occasional single words are clearly related, but the language
patterns are poles apart. *English is a Germanic tongue, not an
Italic.*

The decisive event, more than anything else, that changed
Old English to Middle English was the Norman Conquest, which

was irreversible after the Norman victory over the Saxons at Hastings in 1066. Middle English has been aptly if oversimply described as the issue of the marriage of Old English and Old French. Again, without minute analysis, the lines from Chaucer's *Canterbury Tales* (about 1400), describing the Wife of Bath, may prove instructive for our purpose if compared to a Modern English version.[5]

Her kerchiefs were of finely woven ground;
Hir coverchiefs ful fyne were of ground;

I dared have sworn they weighed a good ten pound,
I dorste swere they weyeden ten pound

The ones she wore on Sunday, on her head.
That on a Sunday weren upon hir heed.

Her hose were of the finest scarlet red
Hir hosen weren of fyn scarlet reed,

And gartered tight; her shoes were soft and new.
Ful streite yteyd, and shoes ful moyste and newe.

Bold was her face, handsome, and red in hue.
Boold was hir face, and fair, and reed of hewe.

A worthy woman all her life, what's more:
She was a worthy woman all hir lyve:

She'd had five husbands, all at the church door,
Housbondes at chirche dore she hadde fyve,

Apart from other company in youth;
Withouten oother compaignye in youthe,—

No need just now to speak of that, forsooth:
But thereof nedeth nat to speke as nowthe.

Chaucer's English, though much closer to ours than Old English, still cannot be read properly in the original without special study. But to an ear attuned to its melodies, it can be a joy and a delight.

Just as no one knows anything precise about the earliest beginnings of language, so no one knows precisely why language changes. Change in itself, however, is almost a law of language; no language has ever remained the same in all respects even from one generation to the next. Historical changes in the Indo-European family have been closely studied, the changes in English particularly. The *how* and the *when* can be fairly well pinpointed; the *why* eludes us. Change does occur; linguistic change is a fact of life that must be accepted. There is hardly a more wasteful activity than resistance to normal change in a language.

American English is different in many respects from British English or Australian English, even from Canadian English, on the same continent. American linguistic uniqueness began to develop before the American Revolution. Our language remains unique today, especially in intonation, the melody and rhythm of utterances. Moreover, there is no American equivalent of Received Standard English, nor of the rigid British class and regional dialects. In our country there are several regional dialects of equal prestige, and no sharp line divides cultured from common speech. The dialects of most Americans differ only in relatively minor respects, while the underlying linguistic characteristics are pretty much the same. Every native American can understand the language of nearly every other native American. When the language is reduced to print, many local differences disappear, though this is no doubt in part because written English is a generalized national and even international means of communication. Written English may be thought of, in fact, almost as a special dialect in itself.

This brings us round again to reading, the central concern of this book: reading is first and foremost a language process. Any language process may best be studied integrally with the signaling system or code that transmits meaning. Reading depends on auding and speaking and is closely linked to writing; auding and speaking are audio-lingual processes, reading and writing are manual-visual, but all are language processes. Speaking and auding may be thought of as sending and receiving operations of audio-lingual communication; writing and reading as sending and receiving operations of communication—"graphics." All four activities are integrally related processes of the total complex language system. They may be analyzed and studied quite apart from the messages sent and received. This is not to deny the importance of the messages, or meanings; on the contrary, the only reason for mastering the language system is to gain ready and easy access to the universe of thought. "A savage, after all, is simply a human organism that has not received enough news from the human race."[6]

Language, then, is the uniquely distinguishing mark of man's humanity: of man's kinship with himself. Man communicates and interacts immediately through his double-symbol systems of speech and print—books, newspapers, magazines, radio, television, movies—all the mass media; he communicates also across barriers and vast stretches of time and space, from generation to generation, from culture to culture, from age to age. Fostering this communication is a function of our libraries, our teachers, and our schools.

Language embraces the spectrum of creative and reflective "mind," from pure mathematics to pure poetry. At one pole of thought, the mathematician is able to say, as cold and clear and beautiful as ice,

$$a^2 + b^2 = c^2$$

or, with Einstein and a host of nuclear physicists,

$$E = mc^2$$

out of which may come, in time, more things in heaven and earth than are dreamt of in our philosophy, or our nightmares. At the opposite pole of emotion, the poet is able to say:

> **Lay me on an anvil, O God.**
> **Beat me and hammer me into a crowbar.**[7]

or:

> **Tiger, tiger, burning bright**
> **In the forests of the night . . . .**[8]

Yet perhaps we should also recall that it was a poet who attempted to span the distance between:

> **Euclid alone has looked on Beauty bare . . . .**[9]

The whole sweep of language, thought, and literature lies between these antipodes—the language of children at play, the workaday talk of us all, great lectures and orations, scientific prose, general essays, fiction, drama, poetic prose, poetry itself.

Imaginative literature, humanistic, reflects life, is a living member of life, interprets life, criticizes and evaluates life. It embodies in permanent forms the insights and the wisdom of the world. The best in literature can broaden, deepen, and enrich life, provided the reader learns how to mine its rich ores. Literature does not come knocking at dark doorways, seeking the sleepers. It must be sought out, stalked, captured, mastered.

It must be deeply read.

Notes to text

Notes to introduction

1. George L. Trager and Henry Lee Smith, Jr., *An Outline of English Structure (Studies in Linguistics:* Occasional Papers, No. 3), Norman, Okla., Battenburg Press, 1951; reprinted, American Council of Learned Societies, Washington, D.C., 1957.
2. Carl A. Lefevre, "Reading Instruction Related to Primary Language Learnings: A Linguistic View," a paper read at the Golden Anniversary Convention of the National Council of Teachers of English, Chicago, Nov. 25, 1960, *The Journal of Developmental Reading,* Spring, 1961, pp. 147–158; Carl A. Lefevre, "Language Patterns and their Graphic Counterparts: A Linguistic View," a paper read at the Sixth Annual Convention of the International Reading Association, St. Louis, May 6, 1961, *Changing Concepts of Reading Instruction: International Reading Association Conference Proceedings,* vol. 6, pp. 245–249, 1961.
3. Doris H. Flinton, *A Three-year Research Project in Beginning Reading and Language Teaching,* Bethlehem Central Schools, Delmar, N.Y., 1961. (A mimeographed report.) Based on the work of I. A. Richards and Christine Gibson, the language emphasis in the reading lessons is semantic rather than structural; yet a number of aspects of this research support suggestions made in this book. Refer to chap. 1, p. 7, for a pertinent observation made by Mrs. Flinton, and to note 2 on p. 201.
   Ruby Kelley (principal investigator), *A Study to Identify the Content of Linguistically Based Grammar Instruction of a Junior High School,* Westport, Conn., June, 1962. (A mimeographed report.) Miss Kelley is reading consultant at the Longlots Junior High School in Westport.
   Ruth G. Strickland, "The Language of Elementary School Children: Its Relationship to the Language of Reading Textbooks and the Quality of Reading of Selected Children," *Bulletin of the School of Education,* vol. 38, no. 4, Indiana University, Bloomington, Ind., July, 1962.

Notes to chapter 1 A program for applying structural linguistics to reading instruction: a preview and guide to this book

1. Grace M. Fernald, *Remedial Techniques in Basic School Subjects*, McGraw-Hill Book Company, Inc., New York, 1943, p. 176.
2. Letter of May 15, 1961. Mrs. Flinton is a reading consultant and director of a three-year state-aided experiment in primary language-teaching methods being conducted by the Bethlehem Central School District, Delmar, N.Y. Her letter was a comment on a talk delivered by the author of this book at the Sixth Annual Conference of the International Reading Association on May 6, 1961, in St. Louis. His paper, "Language Patterns and Their Graphic Counterparts: A Linguistic View of Reading," appears in *Changing Concepts of Reading Instruction: International Reading Association Conference Proceedings*, vol. 6, 1961.
3. Fernald, *Remedial Techniques in Basic School Subjects*, p. 54.

Notes to chapter 2 The reading problem in America

1. May 5, 1960, p. 1, col. 7. Copyright by *The New York Times*. Reprinted by permission.
2. Cited by Paul Witty and David Kopel, *Reading and the Educative Process*, Ginn and Company, Boston, 1939, p. 167.
3. Guy Bond and Miles Tinker, *Reading Difficulties: Their Diagnosis and Correction*, Appleton-Century-Crofts, Division of Meredith Publishing Company, Des Moines, Iowa, 1957, pp. 78–79.
4. Glenn M. Blair, *Diagnostic and Remedial Teaching*, rev. ed., The Macmillan Company, New York, 1956, chap. 2.
5. Cited by Paul Witty, *Reading in Modern Education*, D. C. Heath and Company, Boston, 1949, p. 178.
6. *Ibid.*, pp. 181–182.
7. *Ibid.*, p. 183.
8. Quoted by Paul Witty in "The Improvement of Reading Abilities," *Fifty-fifth Yearbook of the National Society for the Study of Education, Part II*, Chicago, 1956, p. 252.

Notes to chapter 3 The child's language from cradle to kindergarten

1. Strictly speaking, the vocal folds close in conjunction with closure of the epiglottis above them, which covers the opening of the windpipe during swallowing.

2. John McKelway, in the *Washington Evening Star*, Nov. 25, 1960. Reprinted in *The New Republic*, Jan. 2, 1961. Reprinted by permission from John M. McKelway. The rest of the text follows:

   Here comes mother. Mother and father, Bobby and Jack, are in the garden looking for something.

   Here comes Ted. Here comes Eunice. Here comes Pat. Here comes Peter. Here comes Sargent. Here comes Jackie.

   They are all in the garden looking for the mandate.

   Who has the mandate?

   Where is the mandate?

   What color is the mandate?

   Is the mandate large or small?

   Who had the mandate?

   Dwight David had the mandate. He had the mandate for eight years. He got the mandate from Harry. Harry got the mandate from Franklin. Herbert lost the mandate and gave it to Franklin. Calvin had given it to Herbert.

   It is hard to keep the mandate. It is hard to get your hands on it.

   Dwight David tried to give it to Richard.

   Did Richard get the mandate?

   Does Richard have the mandate?

   Is Richard hiding the mandate that belongs to Jack?

   Does the mandate really belong to Jack?

   If the mandate belongs to Jack, why doesn't Richard give it to Jack?

   Maybe Richard doesn't know he has the mandate.

   Does Richard think Jack has the mandate?

   Who has the mandate?

   Does Jack need the mandate? If Jack, or father, or mother, or Jackie, or Ted, or Bobby, or Eunice, or Sargent, find the mandate what will they do with it?

Look.
Look and see.
See Baby Caroline. Here comes Baby Caroline.
No one is watching Baby Caroline. They are all looking for the mandate in the garden.
Baby Caroline has two ducks.
Wait!
Baby Caroline has the mandate!
Look. She is feeding the mandate to the ducks.

Notes to chapter 4   Intonation: the melodies of the printed page

1. John Ciardi, "Christmas Greetings to the American Dream," *Saturday Review*, Dec. 23, 1961, p. 27.

Notes to chapter 6   Structure words

1. E. W. Dolch, *The Basic Sight Word Test*, The Garrard Press, Champaign, Ill., 1942. Reprinted by permission from Garrard Press.
2. Edward Fry, "Teaching a Basic Vocabulary," *Elementary English*, April, 1960, p. 41. Lists reprinted by permission from Dr. Edward Fry and from Learning through Seeing, Inc.
3. *Ibid.*, p. 38.

Notes to chapter 8   Spelling, word analysis, and phonics

1. Ivah Green, "All Words Belong to First Graders," *Elementary English*, October, 1959, pp. 383–384. Reprinted by permission from Ivah Green.
2. Grace M. Fernald, *Remedial Techniques in Basic School Subjects*, McGraw-Hill Book Company, Inc., New York, 1943, pp. 105, 108, 115.

Notes to chapter 9   The import of language and of reading

1. Walt Whitman, *Slang in America*, 1885. Quoted in H. L. Mencken, *A New Dictionary of Quotations*, Alfred A. Knopf, Inc., New York, 1960, p. 649.
2. 1828. Quoted in Mencken, *loc. cit.*
3. *Language: A Linguistic Introduction to History*, translated by Paul Rodin, Routledge & Kegan Paul, Ltd., London, 1925.
4. *Ibid.*, p. 11.
5. The modern English is from the translation by Nevill Coghill, *The Canterbury Tales*, Penguin Books, Inc., Baltimore, 1952. Reprinted by permission from John Farquharson, Ltd.
6. John Ciardi, "Literature Undefended," *Saturday Review*, Jan. 31, 1959.
7. Carl Sandburg, "Prayers of Steel."
8. William Blake, "The Tiger."
9. Edna St. Vincent Millay, "Sonnet."

Appendix A: Summary of symbols and abbreviations

Contents

A. Four Sentence Functions

B. Four Important Sentence Patterns

Two Important Sentence Pattern Transformations
(passive constructions)

C. Four Word Classes: Noun, Verb, Adjective, Adverb

Word-form Changes (inflections)

D. Nonsegmental Phonemes (Trager-Smith "suprasegmental")

Pitch
  Pitch Contour
Stress
Juncture

E. Segmental Phonemes

Simple Vowels (short vowels)
  The Three Semivowels
Complex Vowel Nuclei (long vowels and diphthongs)
Consonants (arranged in pairs, voiced and voiceless)
  "Nasal Continuant" Consonants (also "nasal resonants")
  "Liquid" Consonants (also "lateral resonants")

A. FOUR SENTENCE FUNCTIONS

N	Noun function
V	Verb function (**Lv** signifies linking-verb function)
A	Adjective function
Ad	Adverb function

B. FOUR IMPORTANT SENTENCE PATTERNS

1. **N V**
   N V A
   N V Ad

2. **N V N**

3. **N V N N**

4. **N Lv N**
   N Lv A
   N Lv Ad

Two Important PATTERN TRANSFORMATIONS
    (passive constructions)

1. **N vV** (v signifies verb marker in the passive construction)
2. **N vV by N** (**by N** signifies agency in the passive construction)

C. FOUR WORD CLASSES: NOUN, VERB, ADJECTIVE, ADVERB

N	Noun class
V	Verb class
A	Adjective class
Ad	Adverb class

WORD-FORM CHANGES (inflections)

Noun	**N**	(base)
	N-s/es	(plural)
	N-'s/s'	(genitive)
Verb parts	**V**	(base)
	V-s/es	(third person singular)
	V-ed	(past)
	V-ing	(present participle)
	V-ed/en	(past participle)
Adjective	**A/Ad**	(base)
and	**A/Ad-er**	(comparative)
Adverb	**A/Ad-est**	(superlative)

(Some adjectives and some adverbs take the above inflections. The suffix -ly commonly marks an adverb derived from an adjective, but -ly also marks common adjectives: *lovely, manly.* A large number of derivational prefixes and suffixes mark both adjectives and adverbs.)

D. NONSEGMENTAL PHONEMES (Trager-Smith *suprasegmental*)
   Pitch: *Four significant levels (or ranges)*

l	low
n	normal
h	high
hh	extra high

Pitch contour

A pitch contour is a broken-line graph representing significant pitch changes in an utterance.

Stress: *Four significant degrees*

/	heavy
∧	medium
\	light
ᴜ	weak

Juncture: *Four significant ways of interrupting or terminating the voice stream*

+   open juncture: separates some words and syllables.

→   level terminal: terminates some syntactical elements within utterances.

↗   fade-rise terminal: terminates some syntactical elements within utterances; also terminates some questions.

↘   fade-fall terminal: terminates statements and commands; it is the characteristic termination of many questions; generally signifies finality, the termination of an utterance.

Simple vowels (short vowels)

/ æ /	the vowel phoneme in *pat*
/ e /	the vowel phoneme in *pet*
/ i /	the vowel phoneme in *pit*
/ a /	the vowel phoneme in *pot*
/ ə /	the vowel phoneme in *but* (schwa sound)
/ u /	the vowel phoneme in *put*
/ ɔ /	the vowel phoneme in *taught*
/ ɨ /	the first vowel phoneme in *below*
	(/ ɨ / and / ə / appear frequently in weak-stressed syllables; they are often interchangeable, even in the speech of the same speaker, depending on the articulatory and phonemic environment, including pitch and stress variations)
/ o /	the initial vowel phoneme in the complex vowel nucleus / ow / as in *go;* rarely uttered as a simple vowel by itself in American English.

The three semivowels

/ h /	the initial phoneme in *hem*
/ w /	the initial phoneme in *wet*
/ y /	the initial phoneme in *yet*

When semivowels occur initially as in the examples above, they are frequently represented in writing and print by letters corresponding to their respective phonemic symbols. Otherwise—except as the second sound in the diphthongs spelled *ou, ow* and *oi, oy* (/ aw / and / oy / or / ɔy /)—semivowel phonemes are not clearly represented by letters in the English graphic system.

Complex vowel nuclei (long vowels and diphthongs)

A complex vowel nucleus is a rapid sequence of vowel phonemes—a simple vowel followed by a semivowel—in which
it is virtually impossible for the ear to note where the simple
vowel ends and the semivowel begins. Native speakers tend
to hear each complex vowel nucleus as a single significant
sound.

/ ey /	the vowel sequence in *pate* (long "*a*")
/ iy /	the vowel sequence in *Pete* (long "*e*")
/ ay /	the vowel sequence in *pike* (long "*i*")
/ ow /	the vowel sequence in *pole* (long "*o*")
/ uw /	the vowel sequence in *pool, rule* (long "*u*")
/ aw /	the vowel sequence in *pound* (diphthong)
/ oy / or / ɔy /	the vowel sequence in *point* (diphthong)

Certain of the above vowel sequences, or complex vowel
nuclei, are the long vowels which are frequently spelled with
single letters; although they are also frequently spelled as
digraphs, or two-letter graphemes, the long vowels have not
been traditionally regarded as diphthongs.

Below is a table showing some of these common spellings of
the long vowels.

Phonemic symbols	Single-letter spellings	Digraphs, or two-letter graphemes
/ ey /	*a*	*ai, ay, ey*
/ iy /	*e*	*ea, ee, ei, ie*
/ ay /	*i, y*	*ei, ie, uy*
/ ow /	*o*	*oa, oo, ow*
/ uw /	*u*	*oo, ou, ue*

Consonants (arranged in voiced and voiceless pairs)

/ b /	(voiced)	the initial phoneme in **bat**
/ p /	(voiceless)	the initial phoneme in **pat**
/ d /	(voiced)	the initial phoneme in **dad**
/ t /	(voiceless)	the initial phoneme in **tap**
/ g /	(voiced)	the initial phoneme in **gap**
/ k /	(voiceless)	the initial phoneme in **cap**
/ v /	(voiced)	the initial phoneme in **vat**
/ f /	(voiced)	the initial phoneme in **fat**
/ z /	(voiced)	the initial phoneme in **zip**
/ s /	(voiceless)	the initial phoneme in **sip**
/ ǰ /	(voiced)	the initial phoneme in **jab**
/ č /	(voiceless)	the initial phoneme in **chap**
/ ð /	(voiced)	the initial phoneme in **this**
/ θ /	(voiceless)	the initial phoneme in **thin**
/ ž /	(voiced)	the medial consonant phoneme in **vision** (/ ž / does not occur initially in English except in the exotic names **Gigi** and **Zha Zha**)
/ š /	(voiceless)	the initial phoneme in **ship**

"Nasal continuant" consonants (also "nasal resonants")

/ *m* /   the initial phoneme in *map*
/ *n* /   the initial phoneme in *nap*
/ ŋ /   the terminal phoneme in *bang* (/ ŋ / does not
                                          occur initially in
                                          English)

"Liquid" consonants (also "lateral resonants")

/ *l* /   the initial phoneme in *lap*
/ *r* /   the initial phoneme in *rap*

Appendix B: The human speech instrument

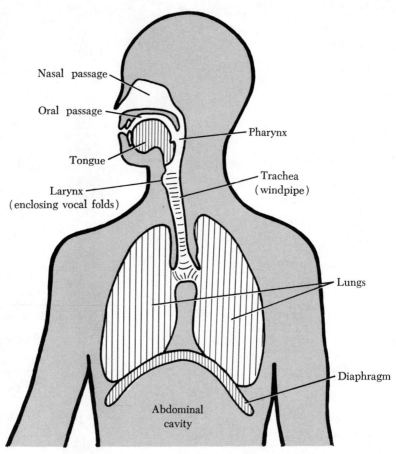

Figure 1a. The Human Speech Instrument

ʍan's physiological means of talking, his so-called speech organs, may be compared, in their function of producing the sounds of language, to a musical wind instrument. In fact, just as hand tools are extensions of the human body, certain musical instruments are extensions of the human speech (and song) instrument. The analogy works both ways. No wonder the comparison of the "organs" of speech with instruments of music comes so readily to mind.

The diaphragm, a powerful layer of muscle between the chest and abdominal cavities, aided by the abdominal muscles and the

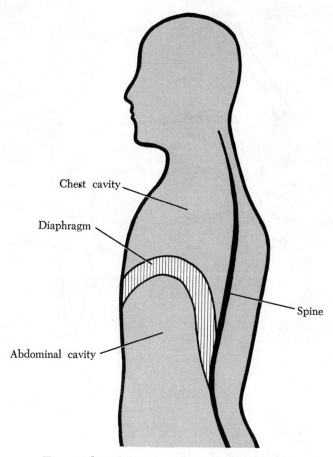

Chest cavity

Diaphragm

Spine

Abdominal cavity

Figure 1*b*. Side Section Showing Diaphragm

muscles that expand and contract the rib cage, gives a bellows action to the lungs in breathing. The expulsion of breath, upward through the trachea and through the opening controlled by the vocal folds in the larynx, carries the vocal sound that even very young children learn to articulate as speech. This stream of speech issues largely from the oral opening but also from the nasal openings. For a simple, generalized view, see Figure 1*a*, "The Human Speech Instrument," and Figure 1*b*, "Side Section Showing Diaphragm."

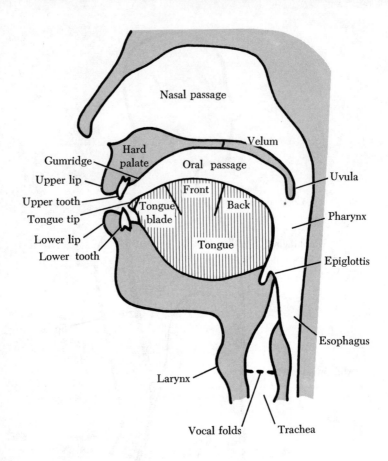

Figure 2. The Speech Mechanism

The vocal folds are somewhat comparable in their action to the double reed in the mouthpiece of an oboe or bassoon; their vibrations produce the significant pitch levels of our speech tunes. The tongue is a powerful muscle, rather a complex mass of integrated muscles, capable of an intricate specificity of actions, shaping and modulating the stream of vocal sound. Variations in the overall height of the tongue in the oral passage, the position of the highest part of the tongue, the shape of the upper surface of the tongue, the relative tenseness or laxness of the tongue; variations in the position of the lips; variations in the relative closure or openness of the nasal passage; variations in the muscular movements and actions within the pharynx and the larynx, including the action of the vocal folds—all these elements in various combinations contribute to the articulation of the vowel sounds of language. The figurative comparison of the action of the vocal folds and double reeds should not be taken literally, of course.

Consonant sounds are generally formed in one of three ways: (1) by a stoppage of the stream of vocal sound at some definite point of articulation; (2) by a muscular constriction producing friction over some definite surface within the oral passage; or (3) by a definite modification of the combined resonance of the oral and nasal passages; these three kinds of consonant sounds are called (1) **stops**, (2) **fricatives**, and (3) **continuants**, or **resonants**. Stops include /b/, /p/, /d/, /t/, /g/, /k/, /ǰ/, /č/; fricatives include /v/, /f/, /z/, /s/, /ž/, /š/, /ð/, /θ/; nasal continuants, or resonants, include /m/, /n/, /ŋ/; /l/ and /r/ are lateral resonants. Resonants are all voiced; both stops and fricatives contrast in voiced and voiceless pairs. Figure 2, "The Speech Mechanism," is a simple presentation of the organs of the throat and head that are capable of making all the basic speech sounds.

The simplified explanation given here uses data from both **articulatory** and **acoustic** phonetics, but adapts this information to a presentation of the means by which American English pho-

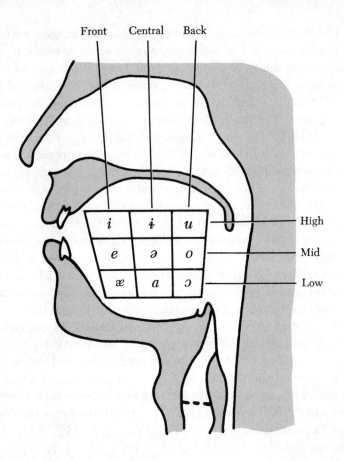

Figure 3. The Vowel Trapezoid (approximate position in mouth)

nemes are produced. The discussion focuses on **phonemics** rather than **phonetics,** and concerns itself mainly with the vowels. The dialect is that of the author, a native of the Midwest, who has lived most of his life in Michigan, Minnesota, and Illinois.

The actual, detailed processes of speech are much more intricate, and are capable of more precise description than this simplified explanation can suggest; nevertheless this explanation is essentially true in its presentation of the main concepts needed for a broad grasp of the way the sounds of language are produced. It may be helpful to think of the segmental phonemes as significant points, or nodes, in the vocal stream that emerges from the lips of native speakers: to a certain extent, every phoneme blends, or merges, with the phoneme going before it or coming after. Yet the native ear groups similar sounds together into the distinctive and significant classes we recognize as phonemes. And despite the notorious irregularities of the English spelling system, the alphabetical principle broadly applies to the relationship of phonemes to spelling, particularly in writing as distinct from reading; both handwriting and typing must be spelled out, laboriously, one letter at a time.

The simple vowel phonemes of American English lend themselves to a symmetrical arrangement according to the position of the tongue within the oral passage during the articulation of each vowel sound. If we think of the head in cross section, we may visualize the oral cavity as a vowel trapezoid (also called a triangle or quadrangle). This trapezoid divides neatly into three subsections from front to back, and into three subsections from high to low. Vowels may thus be designated front, central, and back, as well as high, mid, and low; both sets of terms are used to designate the simple vowel sounds. For example, $/i/$ is a high front vowel; $/a/$ a low central vowel; and $/o/$ is a mid back vowel. Figure 3, "The Vowel Trapezoid," is a generalized drawing that shows the approximate position of the vowel trapezoid and its nine subsections in the oral passage.

Figures 4, 5, and 6 show relative tongue positions for the front, central, and back vowels, respectively, with a curving line at each of the high, mid, and low positions. Each curve represents the top, or profile, of the tongue in each position, nine positions all told. Such curves may be called *tongue lines.* Each of these three drawings approximates three relative positions of the tongue in position to articulate three phonemes formed by successive lowered or raised positions of the tongue.

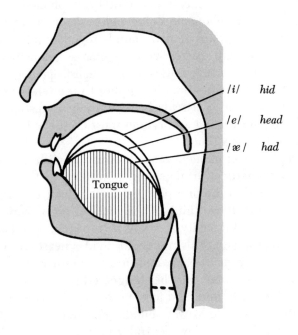

/i/   hid

/e/   head

/æ/   had

Tongue

Figure 4. Simple Front Vowels:/ *i*/, /*e*/, / *æ* / (as in *hid,
head, had*)

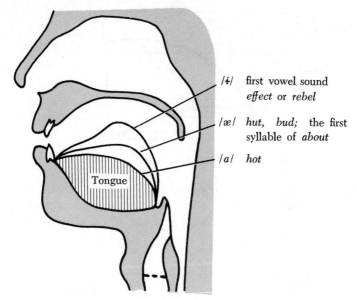

/ɨ/   first vowel sound *effect* or *rebel*

/æ/   *hut, bud;* the first syllable of *about*

/a/   *hot*

Tongue

Figure 5. Simple Central Vowels: /ɨ/, /æ/, /a/ (as in the first syllable of *effect* or *rebel*; *hut, bud,* the first syllable of *about*; *hot*)

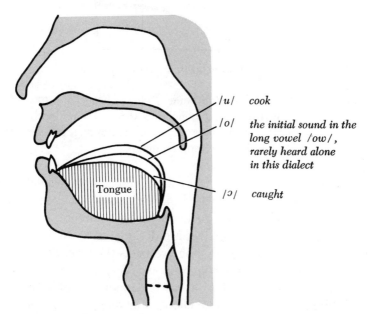

/u/   *cook*

/o/   *the initial sound in the long vowel /ow/, rarely heard alone in this dialect*

/ɔ/   *caught*

Tongue

Figure 6. Simple Back Vowels: / u /, / o /, / ɔ / (as in *cook*; the initial sound in the long vowel / ow /, rarely heard alone in this dialect; *caught*)

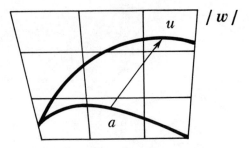

A low central to high back vowel sequence

Figure 7. The *ow/ou* diphthong / *aw* / (*cow, south, grout*). The semivowel / *w* / concludes this sequence with a distinctive rounding of the lips and narrowing of the oral passage by the tongue.

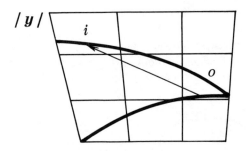

A mid back to high front vowel sequence

Figure 8. The *oy/oi* diphthong / *oy* / (*boy, coil, toy*). The semivowel / *y* / concludes this sequence with a flattening of the lips and a near stoppage of the voice stream by the tongue blade.

In the author's dialect, there are seven **complex vowel nuclei,** or vowel sequences, articulated in continuous gliding movements from one vowel position to another. In common "lay" terminology, these vowel sequences are designated as *diphthongs* and *long vowels.* One common usage restricts the term *diphthong* to / *aw* / as in *south* and *cow,* and to / *oy* / in *boy* and *coil:* a diphthong is thought of as a vowel sequence regularly spelled with two letters: / *aw* / is spelled *ou* or *ow;* / *oy* / is spelled *oy* or *oi*. The long vowels, on the contrary, though they may be spelled with two letters in some words, are thought of as "the long sounds" of the letters *a, e, i, o* and *u*. Both *diphthong* and *long vowel* in such usage probably derive from phonics, because these terms reflect a confusion of sound with spelling. A diphthong is considered to be a sequence of two vowel sounds, but a long vowel only one vowel sound. Both are in fact complex vowel nuclei. See Figures 7, 8, 9, 10, 11, 12, and 13.

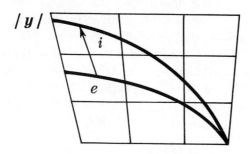

A mid front to high front vowel sequence

Figure 9. The long *a* sound. / *ey* / (*bait, great, grate*). The semivowel / *y* / concludes this sequence with a flattening of the lips and a near stoppage of the voice stream by the tongue blade.

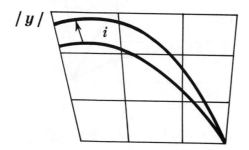

A high front to high(er) front vowel sequence

Figure 10. The long *e* sound: / *iy* / (*beet, meat, grebe, greet*). The semivowel / *y* / concludes this sequence with a flattening of the lips and a near stoppage of the voice stream by the tongue blade.

Although heard by the native ear as a single sound, each long vowel is actually a sequence of two phonemes uttered in such rapid succession that it is nearly impossible to hear when one leaves off and the other begins. It may be easier to feel the gliding action of the tongue than it is to hear the shifting vowel sound. Such vowel sequences, or complex vowel nuclei, are produced during a definite movement of the tongue from one position to another, and are often accompanied by a distinctive and significant degree of rounding of the lips, which further modifies the quality of the vowel sounds. Illustrations in this text represent these vowel sequences by means of two curves representing the tongue profile at the beginning and at the end of its action during articulation. An arrow between the tongue lines in each figure points the direction of the tongue action. The relative rounding of the lips, not illustrated, is an important third variable feature in the articulation of these complex vowel nuclei. See Figures 7, 8, 9, 10, 11, 12, and 13.

/ y /

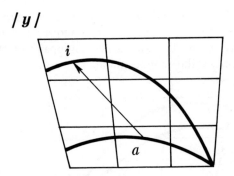

A low central to high front vowel sequence

Figure 11. The long *i* sound: / *ay* / (*bite, might, gripe*). The semivowel / *y* / concludes this sequence with a flattening of the lips and a near stoppage of the voice stream by the tongue blade.

/ w /

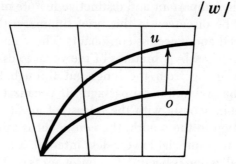

A mid back to high back vowel sequence

Figure 12. The long *o* sound: / *ow* / (*boat, mode, growth*). The semivowel / *w* / concludes this sequence with a distinctive rounding of the lips and a narrowing of the oral passage by the tongue.

/ w /

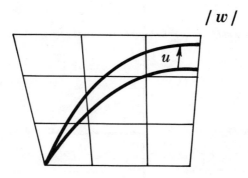

A high back to high(er) back vowel sequence

Figure 13. The long *u* sound: / *uw* / (*boot, soup, fruit*). The semivowel / *w* / concludes this sequence with a distinctive rounding of the lips and a narrowing of the oral passage by the tongue.

One other important and distinctive feature of speech sounds remains to be discussed in this brief summary: the contrast between voiced and voiceless consonants. The sound of the human voice is produced by vibrations of the vocal folds and carried by the breath, going from the lungs out through the larynx, the pharynx, the oral and nasal passages. If vocalization, or voicing, occurs simultaneously with the release of air at a definite point of articulation in the mouth, the consonant is said to be voiced. If there is an appreciable voiceless interval, a quick puff of air, before vocalization is begun, the consonant is said to be voiceless. This is the distinctive contrast between / *ba* / (voiced) and / *pa* / (voiceless). If the syllable begins with / *m* /, vocalization, audible through the nasal passages, begins before the lips are parted to release the voice stream. Such a "prevocalized consonant," so to speak, is a nasal continuant, or resonant; / *b* / and / *p* / are stops. Figure 14 is a graphic abstraction of these contrasts. In the same

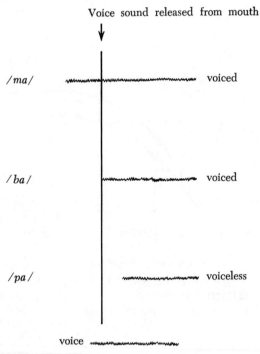

Figure 14. Consonant Contrasts: /*ma*/, /*ba*/, /*pa*/

228   *Linguistics and the teaching of reading*

graphic style, Figure 15 illustrates two other voiced-voiceless contrasting pairs: */ da /* and */ ta /*; and */ ga /* and */ ka /*. Actually, the voiced-voiceless contrast is not quite this simple if measured by laboratory equipment, or even when attended to by a trained ear, but there is such a contrast in this dialect. It is phonemically distinctive and significant.

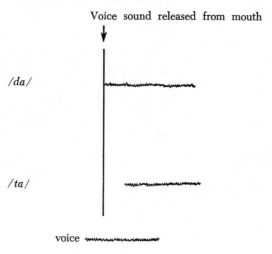

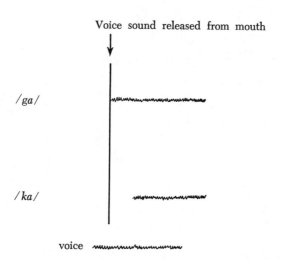

Figure 15. Consonant Contrasts: */da/, /ta/; /ga/, /ka/*

Selected bibliography

readers of *Linguistics and the Teaching of Reading* who want
to go further in linguistics and closely related fields may find
what they seek in the classified lists presented in this Appendix.
These lists are neither inclusive nor directive; they are highly
selective. As an avenue into the study of linguistics, a work that
is accessible and illuminating to one reader may seem difficult
and obscure to another. The best approach is a free and easy
selection of readings that appear attractive, reserving the right
always to put aside one book for another until intellectual familiarity is achieved. In the early stages of the game, one man's meat
may be another man's poison. One reader may approach by the
easy stages of periodical articles or a book of essays; another may
want to sink his teeth directly into Bloomfield's *Language*. Still
others, mainly interested in American English for native Americans, may find their best guidance in works designed for teaching
English as a foreign language. In time, however, a student of
linguistics should be able to read almost anything in the field
with some profit. At first, the problem is simply how to get
started and keep going.

For these reasons, this selected bibliography is classified as
follows:
1. Periodicals
2. Books valuable as introductions (annotated)
   Books not recommended (annotated)
3. Primary sources of data and interpretation
4. A supplementary list
5. A list of traditional works

Periodicals

Current issues as well as back files of these periodicals are valuable sources of discussions for persons seeking an introduction to
linguistics, to its practical applications, and to the debated and
sometimes controversial issues of educational linguistics.

American Speech, Columbia University Press, New York.

College Composition and Communication, National Council of Teachers of English, Champaign, Ill.

College English, National Council of Teachers of English, Champaign, Ill.

Elementary English, National Council of Teachers of English, Champaign, Ill.

The English Journal, National Council of Teachers of English, Champaign, Ill.

General Linguistics, Department of Modern Foreign Languages, University of Kentucky, Lexington, Ky.

Hexagon, an interdisciplinary journal, Chicago Teachers College North, Chicago.

International Journal of American Linguists, C. F. Voegelin (ed.), Indiana University, Bloomington, Ind.

Journal of Developmental Reading, Purdue University, Lafayette, Ind.

Journal of Speech and Hearing Research, American Speech and Hearing Association, Washington.

Language, Yale University, New Haven, Conn.

Language Learning, Rackham Building, Ann Arbor, Mich.

Publications of the Modern Language Association, Modern Language Association of America, New York.

The Quarterly Journal of Speech, Louisiana State University, Baton Rouge, La.

Word, Linguistic Society of America, Austin, Texas.

Books valuable as introductions: an annotated list

Allen, Harold B. (ed.): *Readings in Applied English Linguistics,* Appleton-Century-Crofts, Division of Meredith Publishing Company, Des Moines, Iowa, 1958. The first collection of articles (sixty-five) for laymen and classroom teachers from linguistic and professional journals; revised edition scheduled for publication.

Brooks, Nelson: *Language and Language Learning: Theory and Practice.* Harcourt, Brace & World, Inc., New York, 1960. A comprehensive and well-written small book, especially for readers interested in foreign language teaching; valuable for clear presentation of basic questions, definitions of terms, and focus on educational issues.

Brown, Dona Worrall, Wallace C. Brown, and Dudley Bailey, *Form in Modern English,* Oxford University Press, New York, 1958. A freshman textbook incorporating elements of the linguistic analysis, but omitting intonation entirely; introduces new definitions for traditional terminology.

Encyclopaedia Britannica; Encyclopedia Americana. The Britannica, the Americana, and other encyclopedias offer excellent articles on linguistics; the reader must exercise scholarly judgment in noting the author's name and sources. Otto Jespersen's essay on language in the Encyclopaedia Britannica, vol. 13, 1929 edition, is a good example. Another is Edward Sapir's famed article on the Indian languages of North America, Encyclopaedia Britannica, vol. 5, 1929 edition.

Fernald, Grace M.: *Remedial Techniques in Basic School Subjects,* McGraw-Hill Book Company, Inc., New York, 1943. Prescientific work by a fine teacher and a well-trained psychologist; readers would do well to study this wise book for its valuable insights and records of successful teaching, and to pay no more attention to the "kinesthetic method" than the author herself does.

Francis, Nelson W.: *The Structure of American English,* The Ronald Press Company, New York, 1958. A compendious book designed for an advanced basic language course in American English; good chapters on linguistics and the teacher, and on American dialects (by Raven McDavid, Jr., a linguistic geographer).

Fries, Charles Carpenter. Professor Fries of the University of Michigan has played a leading role in the United States and in the world in linguistics and the teaching of English, with special attention to teaching English as a second language. The four books described below are his most important for us.

————: *American English Grammar,* Appleton-Century-Crofts, Division of Meredith Publishing Company, Des Moines, Iowa, 1940. A "grammar of usage," this important early work is based on an analysis of thousands of letters in the files of the War Department. It was published as English Monograph No. 10, National Council of Teachers of English.

————: *The Structure of English,* Harcourt, Brace & World, Inc., New York, 1952. The first book to attempt to provide a modern syntax for the layman and classroom teacher; based on, and limited to, about fifty hours of recorded telephone conversations; good on word order, clear on intonation but gives it no prominence. Teachers inexperienced in linguistics find this a difficult book. Nevertheless, this work and the Trager-Smith analysis provide the primary sources for most texts in applied English linguistics.

————: *Teaching and Learning English as a Foreign Language,* The University of Michigan Press, Ann Arbor, Mich., 1948. Pioneer work in its field, valuable because it demonstrates how every language teacher must consciously think about language structure and function in order to teach.

————: *Linguistics and Reading,* Holt, Rinehart and Winston, Inc., New York, 1963. Valuable historical chapters on reading pedagogy and linguistic science. The approach to reading instruction is neo-Bloomfieldian, centering on a programed development of recognition of English spelling patterns.

Roberts, Paul: *English Sentences,* Harcourt, Brace & World, Inc., 1962. An effort to translate Chomsky's *Syntactic Structures* into a high school textbook; the general effect is to present so many sentence patterns that the pattern concept itself becomes blurred. Roberts' most traditional book since *Understanding Grammar* (not listed here).

————: *Patterns of English,* teachers' edition, Harcourt, Brace & World, Inc., New York, 1956. The first linguistically based book for high school students, including much exercise material; probably the most popular treatment so far for laymen and teachers; the teachers' edition contains persuasive discussion of underlying issues, and relates structural grammar to traditional grammar.

————: *Understanding English,* Harper & Row, Publishers, Incorporated, New York, 1958. A clearly but not profoundly written textbook for college freshmen, with workbook; some, though not all, of the virtues of *Patterns of English.*

Smith, Henry Lee: *Linguistic Science and the Teaching of English,* Harvard University Press, Cambridge, Mass., 1956. An Inglis lecture, by the Smith of Trager and Smith, this slim early volume is persuasive in arguing the pertinence of linguistics to the teaching of English, especially writing, spelling, and reading. The emphasis is on phonemics.

Whitehall, Harold: *Structural Essentials of English,* Harcourt, Brace & World, Inc., New York, 1956. A compact presentation of elements of the structural linguistic analysis the author has found applicable to the teaching of composition; very good on the relation of the graphic system to significant elements of pitch, stress, and juncture.

Books not recommended

Concerning two popularly written books on language, listed below, the strictures of Professor Robert Hall, Jr., are well deserved and merit repetition here.

Bodmer, Frederick, and Lancelot Hogben: *The Loom of Language,* W. W. Norton & Company, Inc., New York, 1944.

Pei, Mario A: *The Story of Language,* J. B. Lippincott Company, Philadelphia, 1949.

"Both of these attempts at popularization cater to all the traditional misconceptions we have tried to refute: prescriptive dogmatism, misunderstanding of the relation of writing to language, and ethnocentric value-judgments. Both are pretentious, full of out-of-date notions, misinformation and misinterpretation, and are wholly misleading." (*Linguistics and Your Language,* Robert A. Hall, Jr., Doubleday & Company, Inc., Garden City, N.Y., 1950, p. 263.)

Also not recommended:

Bloomfield, Leonard, and Clarence L. Barnhart: *Let's Read: A Linguistic Approach,* Wayne State University Press, Detroit,

1961. An ambitious, but unfortunately belated presentation of reading materials developed by the late Leonard Bloomfield; largely confined to phonemic analysis, the materials are rigid and artificial, a variation upon the phonics method; no serious consideration of intonation and syntax.

Primary sources of data and interpretation

Atwood, Elmer: *A Survey of Verb Forms in the Eastern United States*, The University of Michigan Press, Ann Arbor, Mich., 1953.

Bloch, Bernard, and G. L. Trager: *Outline of Linguistic Analysis*, Linguistic Society of America, Austin, Tex., 1952.

Bloomfield, Leonard: *Language*, Holt, Rinehart and Winston, Inc., New York, 1933.

Boaz, Franz: *Race, Language, and Culture*, The Macmillan Company, New York, 1940.

Chomsky, Noam: *Syntactic Structures*, Mouton and Company, The Hague, 1957.

Gelb, I. J.: *A Study of Writing: The Foundations of Grammaticology*, The University of Chicago Press, Chicago, 1952.

Gleason, Henry A.: *An Introduction to Descriptive Linguistics*, rev. ed., Holt, Rinehart and Winston, Inc., New York, 1961.

Hall, Robert: "Sounds and Spelling in English," Linguistica, Ithaca, N.Y., 1961.

Harris, Zellig: *Methods in Structural Linguistics*, rev. ed., The University of Chicago Press, Chicago, 1961.

Hill, Archibald A.: *Introduction to Linguistic Structures*, Harcourt, Brace & World, Inc., New York, 1958.

Hockett, Charles F.: *A Course in Modern Linguistics*, The Macmillan Company, New York, 1958.

Hoenigswald, Henry M.: *Language Change and Linguistic Reconstruction*, The University of Chicago Press, Chicago, 1960.

Joos, Martin (ed.): *Readings in Linguistics: The Development of Descriptive Linguistics in America since 1925*, 2d ed., American Council of Learned Societies, New York, 1958.

Kurath, Hans: *Handbook of the Linguistic Geography of New England,* Brown University Press, Providence, R.I., 1939.

———: *A Word Geography of the Eastern United States,* The University of Michigan Press, Ann Arbor, Mich., 1949.

——— and Raven McDavid, Jr.: *The Pronunciation of English in the Atlantic States,* The University of Michigan Press, Ann Arbor, Mich., 1961.

——— (director and editor), and others: *Linguistic Atlas of New England,* Brown University Press, Providence, R.I., 1939, 1943.

Mencken, Henry L.: *American Language,* 4th ed., Alfred A. Knopf, Inc., New York, 1937, and Supplements 1 (1945) and 2 (1948).

The Oxford English Dictionary (OED), 1884–1928; reissued with supplement, 1933; originally entitled *A New English Dictionary on Historical Principles* (NED).

Pike, Kenneth: *The Intonation of American English,* The University of Michigan Press, Ann Arbor, Mich., 1946.

———: *Phonemics: A Technique for Reducing Languages to Writing,* The University of Michigan Press, Ann Arbor, Mich., 1947.

Sapir, Edward: *Language: An Introduction to the Study of Speech,* Harcourt, Brace & World, Inc., New York, 1949 (first edition, 1921), reprinted by Harvest Books, Harcourt, Brace & World, Inc., New York, 1955.

———: *Selected Writings of Edward Sapir,* David G. Mandelbaum (ed.), University of California Press, Berkeley, Calif., 1951.

Trager, George L., and Henry Lee Smith, Jr.: *An Outline of English Structure* (*Studies in Linguistics,* Occasional Papers, No. 3), Battenburg Press, Norman, Okla., 1951; reprinted, American Council of Learned Societies, Washington, D.C., 1957.

A supplementary list

Aiken, Janet Rankin: *A New Plan of English Grammar,* Holt, Rinehart and Winston, Inc., New York, 1933.

————: *Commonsense Grammar,* Thomas Y. Crowell Company, New York, 1936.

————: *English Present and Past,* The Ronald Press Company, New York, 1930.

————: *Why English Sounds Change,* The Ronald Press Company, New York, 1929.

Anderson, William L., and Norman Stageberg: *Introductory Readings on Language,* Holt, Rinehart and Winston, Inc., New York, 1962.

Baugh, Albert C.: *A History of the English Language,* 2d ed., Appleton-Century-Crofts, Division of Meredith Publishing Company, Des Moines, Iowa, 1957.

Bryant, Margaret M.: *Modern English and Its Heritage,* 2d ed., The Macmillan Company, New York, 1962.

Carroll, John B.: *The Study of Language,* Harvard University Press, Cambridge, Mass., 1953.

Dean, Leonard F., and Kenneth G. Wilson: *Essays on Language and Usage,* Oxford University Press, Fair Lawn, N.J., 1959.

De Saussure, Ferdinand: *Course of General Linguistics,* Philosophical Library, Inc., New York, 1959.

Greenberg, Joseph (ed.): *Essays in Linguistics,* The University of Chicago Press, Chicago, 1957.

Hall, Robert A., Jr.: *Linguistics and Your Language,* 2d rev. ed. of *Leave Your Language Alone!,* Doubleday & Company, Inc., Garden City, N.Y., 1960.

Hoijer, Harry (ed.): *Language in Culture: Conference on the Interrelations of Language and Other Aspects of Culture,* The University of Chicago Press, Chicago, 1954.

Hooten, E. A.: *Up from the Ape,* The Macmillan Company, New York, 1946.

Jones, Daniel: *An Outline of English Phonetics,* 6th ed., E. P. Dutton & Co., Inc., New York, 1940.

Kenyon, John Samuel, and T. A. Knott: *A Pronouncing Dictionary of American English,* G. & C. Merriam Company, Springfield, Mass., 1944.

Kroeber, Alfred A., and Clyde Kluckhohn: *Culture: A Critical Review of Concepts and Definitions,* Peabody Museum, Cambridge, Mass., 1952.

Lehmann, W. P.: *Historical Linguistics: An Introduction*, Holt, Rinehart and Winston, Inc., New York, 1961.

Leonard, Sterling A.: *The Doctrine of Correctness in English Usage, 1700–1800*, The University of Wisconsin Press, Madison, Wis., 1929.

Leopold, Werner: *Bibliography of Child Language*, Northwestern University Press, Evanston, Ill., 1952.

Marckwardt, Albert H.: *American English*, Oxford University Press, Fairlawn, N.J., 1958. Second printing.

———: *Introduction to the English Language*, Oxford University Press, Fairlawn, N.J., 1942. Tenth printing, 1956.

——— and Fred G. Walcott: *Facts about Current English Usage*, Appleton-Century-Crofts, Division of Meredith Publishing Company, Des Moines, Iowa, 1938.

Moore, Samuel: *Historical Outlines of English Sounds and Inflections*, rev. by Albert Marckwardt, George Wahr Publishing Company, Ann Arbor, Mich., 1951.

Moorhouse, A. C.: *Writing and the Alphabet*, Cobbett, London, 1946.

Morris, Charles W.: *Signs, Language, and Behavior*, Prentice-Hall, Inc., Englewood Cliffs, N.J., 1946.

Nida, Eugene A.: *Learning a Foreign Language*, Foreign Mission Conference of North America, New York, 1950.

Pedersen, Holgar: *Linguistic Science in the Nineteenth Century*, translated by J. Spargo, Harvard University Press, Cambridge, Mass., 1931.

Pyle, Thomas: *Words and Ways of American English*, Random House, Inc., New York, 1952.

Read, Allan Walker: *English Words with Constituent Elements Having Independent Semantic Value*, The Malone Anniversary Studies, T. A. Kerby and H. B. Woolf (eds.), The Johns Hopkins Press, Baltimore, 1949.

Saporta, Sol: *Psycholinguistics: A Book of Readings*, Holt, Rinehart and Winston, Inc., New York, 1961.

Schlauch, Margaret: *The Gift of Language*, Dover Publications, Inc., New York, 1956.

Sledd, James: *A Short Introduction to English Grammar*, Scott, Foresman and Company, Chicago, 1959.

————and Wilma R. Ebbit: *Dictionaries and That Dictionary*, Scott, Foresman and Company, Chicago, 1962.

Sturtevant, Edgar H.: *An Introduction to Linguistic Science*, Yale University Press, New Haven, Conn., 1947.

————: *Linguistic Change*, The University of Chicago Press, Chicago, 1917.

Thomas, Charles K.: *Introduction to the Phonetics of American English*, The Ronald Press Company, New York, 1958.

————: *Handbook of Speech Improvement*, The Ronald Press Company, New York, 1956.

Vendryes, Joseph: *Language: A Linguistic Introduction to History*, translated by Paul Rodin, Routledge & Kegan Paul, Ltd., London, 1925.

Warfel, Harry R.: *Language: A Science of Human Behavior*, Howard Allen, Inc., Cleveland, 1962.

————: *Noah Webster, Schoolmaster to America*, The Macmillan Company, New York, 1936.

Weinrich, Uriel: *Languages in Contact*, Linguistic Circle of New York, New York, 1953.

Whatmough, Joshua: *Language: A Modern Synthesis*, New American Library of World Literature, Inc., New York, 1956.

Whitehall, Harold: "The English Language," in *Webster's New World Dictionary of the American Language*, Harcourt, Brace & World, Inc., New York, 1963, pp. xv–xxxiv.

Whorf, Benjamin: *Four Articles on Metalinguistics*, U.S. Department of State, 1949.

————: *Language, Thought, and Reality*, John Carroll (ed.), John Wiley & Sons, Inc., New York, 1956.

Wise, Claude M.: *Applied Phonetics*, Prentice-Hall, Inc., Englewood Cliffs, N.J., 1955.

A list of traditional works

Curme, George O.: *English Grammar*, College Outline Series, Barnes & Noble, Inc., New York.

————: *Syntax*, D. C. Heath and Company, Boston, 1931.

Jespersen, Otto: *Essentials of English Grammar*, Holt, Rinehart and Winston, Inc., New York, 1933.

————: *Growth and Structure of the English Language,* 9th ed., Basil Blackwell & Mott, Ltd., Oxford, 1956.

————: *Language: Its Nature, Development and Origin,* George Allen & Unwin, Ltd., London, 1922.

————: *A Modern English Grammar on Historical Principles,* Manksgaard, Copenhagen, 1949.

————: *The Philosophy of Grammar,* George Allen & Unwin, Ltd., London, 1948.

Krapp, George Phillip: *A Comprehensive Guide to Good English,* Rand McNally & Company, Chicago, 1927.

————: *The English Language in America,* Appleton-Century-Crofts, Division of Meredith Publishing Company, Des Moines, Iowa, 1925. (2 vols.)

Long, Ralph B.: *The Sentence and Its Parts: A Grammar of Contemporary English,* University of Chicago Press, Chicago, 1961.

Poutsma, H.: *A Grammar of Late Modern English,* Enven P. Noordhoff, NV, Groningen, Netherlands, 1911, 1926.

Sweet, Henry: *A Handbook of Phonetics,* Clarendon Press, Oxford, 1877.

————: *A New English Grammar,* Clarendon Press, Oxford, 1925.

————: *The Oldest English Texts,* Trubner & Co., London, 1885.

Index

Clauses, adverb, 114–115
  as complete statements, 114
  in compound sentences, 63, 65–66
  concluding, final, 115
  defined, 113
  introductory, 114–115
  without markers, 129
  noun, 95, 114, 129
  restrictive, nonrestrictive, 68–69
Clusters, consonant, 181
  noun, xv, xx
  verb, xv, xx, 107
Commands (*see* Requests)
Commas, 49–51, 61, 64–69
  signaling fade-rise terminals, 49–50
Communication, 37–38, 53, 165, 188, 191, 196
Complex vowel nuclei, xiv–xv, 32, 34, 171, 173–174, 178, 180, 211, 224–227
Compound adverbial phrases, 67
Compound predicates, 66
Compound sentence adjuncts, 67
Compound sentences, 65–66
Compound subjects, 66
Compound words, 45–49
Comprehension, 15, 21, 23, 39, 55, 81, 86, 93, 128, 145
  (*See also* Meaning-bearing patterns; Reading theory; Sentence-level utterances; Sentence sense)
Configurations, of sound, 31, 86, 106–107
  of words in writing and print, 153
Conjunctions, 131–132
  adverbial, 127
  as connectors, 131
  coordinating, 131–132
  correlative, 132
  illative, 127
  subordinating, 127
Conjunctive adverbs, 127
Connectors, 131–132
Consonant clusters, 181
Consonants, xiv, 28–29, 32–34, 167–171, 219, 228–229
  continuant, 28, 33, 147–149, 170–171, 213, 219, 228
  "double," 177–178
  fricative, 219

Consonants, liquid, 148–149, 170–171, 213, 219
  resonant, 213, 219, 228–229
  stop, 28, 33, 147, 148, 219, 228–229
  unvoiced, 147–150
  voiced, 148–150
  voiced-voiceless contrast, 169–170, 212, 219, 228–229
Continuant consonants (*see* Consonants)
Contractions, 151–152
Contrasting **N V N N** patterns, 87–88, 90–91
  call, 87–88
  give, 87–88
  summary, 90–91
Contrasting pairs of phonemes, 34–36, 169–170, 212, 228–229
  voiced and voiceless consonants, 34, 169–170, 212, 228–229
  vowels, 34–36
Contrasting prepositional phrases, 126–127
Contrasting rhyme words, 112–113
Contrasting statements and questions, 103–105
Contrasting word forms, 157
Contrasting word pairs, 45–49
  compound nouns, and noun groups, 47–48
  and verb-adverb groups, 46–47
  nouns, and adjectives, 158
  and verbs, 45–46, 157–158
  with open junctures, 48–49
Controlled vocabulary instruction, 37, 119, 133–141
Coordinating conjunctions, 131–132
Correctness as aim in language arts instruction, 32, 43–44, 176–177
Culture and language, 27, 32, 80, 185–197

DeBoer, Kaulfers, and Miller estimates on reading, 18
Declarative statements, 8–9, 53–55, 82–97
Derivational prefixes, xv–xvi, 145, 160
Derivational suffixes, xv–xvi, 145–147, 157–158, 160–161
Diacritical marks, 173, 178

Intonation, dialectal, 52–53
and graphic system, 8–9, 52–72
high-frequency, normal obligatory, 45–73
defined, 4, 30, 44, 50, 52
interpretive, optional, 8
defined, 4, 30, 50, 52
illustrated, 58–60, 74–75
syntactical, 9, 52–53
Intonation patterns, 45–48, 50–75
commands, requests, 54–55, 57
contrasting word-pairs, 45–48
counting, listing, 50
irony, 59
questions, 54–61
of special intent or emphasis, 59–60
statements, 54–56, 63–72
converted to questions, 58–59
Introductory adverbs, 127
Inversions, 80, 83, 97–102, 111
Isolated words (see Single words)

"Jabberwocky," 161–162
Jespersen, Otto, 190, 241–242
Junctures and terminals summarized, 209

Kernel sentences, 86
Kinesics, 4
defined, 30, 53, 103
Kottmeyer data on reading, 17–18

Language, and culture, 27, 32, 80, 185–197
defined, xii, xix, 27, 43, 161, 187–188, 196
origin, 189
theories on, 190–191
and thought, xxi, 187, 189, 196–197
Language analysis, three levels, xiv–xv
Language arts instruction, xiii, xviii, 4–7, 10–11, 23, 31, 52, 55, 57, 63, 73, 79–115, 119–124, 126–129, 131–141, 145–162, 165–166, 168, 174–179, 183–184
correctness as aim in, 32, 43–44, 176–177
(See also Reading theory; Writing instruction)

Language knowledge, conscious, xix, 6, 35, 43, 72, 83, 123
(See also Linguistic consciousness)
unconscious, 6, 8, 29, 30, 33, 54, 69, 84, 123
Language learning, foreign, xix, 161
native, xix, 31, 44, 50, 73, 102, 123, 161, 184
play spirit in, xix, 29, 31, 48–51, 84, 87, 93–94, 161–162
(See also Child's language learning)
Language-related process (see Reading)
Language skills, interrelations of, xviii–xx, 3–6, 39, 43–44, 52–54, 102–103, 121–122, 165–167, 174–175, 183–184, 188, 191, 196–197
Latin, 123, 192, 193
Lefevre, Helen, x
Letters, 38–39, 165–168, 181–182
"silent," 168, 181–182
"that are not there," 168
Level terminal, 62–64, 68, 209
Linguistic consciousness and unconsciousness, xix, 6, 8, 29–31, 33–35, 43, 54–55, 69, 72, 83–84, 123
Linguistics (linguistic science), xi–xvi, xxi
(See also Selected bibliography)
Linking verbs, 82, 88–91, 94–102, 107, 111, 114–115
Liquid consonants (see Consonants)
Listening (see Auding)
Literacy, vii–viii, xii–xiv, xix–xx, 3, 43, 187
Literature, teaching of, xiii, xiv, 196–197
Long vowels, xiv–xv, 32, 34, 120, 171, 173–174, 178, 180, 211, 224–227
"Look! Look! Someone Is in the Garden," 37–38, 202
Lord's Prayer, King James, Old English, Latin versions, 192–193
Loretan, Dr. Joseph O., 16

"Mairzy Doats," 49
Manual-graphic system (see Manual-visual system)
Manual-visual skills, 184

Sledd, James, xxi, 240
Smith, Henry Lee, Jr., xxi, 234, 238
(See also Trager-Smith analysis)
Sound-spelling relationships, xvii, xx, 3, 6, 11, 147–156, 165–167, 181–184
Speech melodies and rhythms (see Intonation; Melodies of printed page; Sentence tunes)
Speech organs, so-called, 188–189, 215–229
    diaphragm, 188, 216–217
    human speech instrument, 215–229
    larynx, 33, 189
    nasal passage, 216–219
    oral passage, 216–219
    pharynx, 216, 218–219
    tongue, 189, 216, 217–218, 222–226
    trachea, 189, 216–217
    vocal folds, 33, 34, 189, 216–219
    windpipe, 33, 189, 216
Spelling, xx, 21, 38–39, 147–156, 173–184
    and reading, correlation of, 38–39, 165–167, 174–175, 183–184
Spelling instruction, 147–156, 173–184
(See also Language arts instruction)
Spelling method of teaching reading, 21, 38–39, 165
Spelling riddle, circus, 183
    ghoti, 182
    potato, 183
Spelling-sound relationships (see Sound-spelling relationships)
Starters, 131
Statements, 9, 54–56
(See also Sentence patterns)
Stop consonants (see Consonants)
Stream of speech (flow of speech, voice stream), xvii, 28–29, 33, 45, 61–64, 91, 165, 167, 217, 219, 221, 228–229
Stress, four significant degrees, 69–75
    summary of, 71, 209
Structure words, xvi, 9–10, 80–81, 117–142
    defined, xvi, 80–81
Subject-verb-complement pattern, 81–82
Subordinating conjunctions, 127

Substitutions, 80, 83, 107, 114–115, 146–147
Syllabication (see Syllables)
Syllables, 174, 177–178, 228–229
    defined, 177
    in oral reading and speech, 174, 177–178, 228–229
    in print and writing, 177–178
Syntactical function order (see Sentence functions and function order)
Syntax, xv
(See also Sentence functions and function order)

Terminals (see Fade-fall terminal; Fade-rise terminal; Junctures and terminals; Level terminal; Open juncture)
"Tetragraphs," 179
Third person singular, 85, 152
Tongue lines, 218, 220, 222–227
Trager, George L., xxi, 237, 238
Trager-Smith analysis, xiv–xv
Transformations, 80, 83, 91–97, 111
Traxler's 1946 testing, 18
Trigraphs, 167, 179

Vendryes, Joseph, 191
Verb-adverb groups, 46–47, 156
Verb clusters, xv, xx
    defined, 107
Verb function, 84–102, 107–111, 114–115
Verb groups, xv, xx, 102, 106–109
    defined, 108–109
Verb headwords, 108–109
Verb inflections, 152–156, 208
Verb markers, 92–94, 100–102, 105–109, 119, 123–126
Verb positions, 5
Verb uses, 70
Verb word class, 147
    five-part, 153–154
    four-part, 153–155
    regular, 152–153
    three-part, 154
Verbals, 107
Verbs, irregular forms, 36

Visual perception, xi, xvii, 119
Vocabulary method, 21, 23, 37, 80, 119–120, 141, 161
(*See also* Single words; Word method)
Vocal folds, 33, 34, 189, 216–219
Vocal qualifiers, 52–54
(*See also* Paralanguage)
Vocal symbol system, primary, xii, xix, 27, 30, 39, 191
(*See also* Audio-lingual system)
Vocalization (voicing), 28, 33–34, 219, 228–229
(*See also* Consonants)
Vowel trapezoid, 220–221, 224–227
Vowels (*see* Short vowels; Simple vowels)

Warfel, Harry R., xxi, 241
Webster, Noah, 189–190
Whitehall, Harold, xxi, 236
Whole-sentence method, vii–viii, xviii–xx, 121–124, 129, 145–147
(*See also* Meaning-bearing patterns; Reading theory; Sentence-level utterances; Sentence sense)
Whorf, Benjamin, xxi, 241
Witty, Paul, 18
Word analysis, 143–184, 219–229
Word bases, xv, 11
(*See also* Adjectives; Adverbs; Morphemes; Nouns; Verbs; Word classes)
Word calling, xvii–xviii, 5–6, 23, 54–55, 107–108
(*See also* Intonation; Single words; Word method; Word-by-word reading)

Word classes (form classes, word-form classes), 81, 83, 145–147
(*See also* Adjectives; Adverbs; Morphemes; Nouns; Verb word class; Verbs)
Word distribution, 81, 83, 129, 145–147
Word-form changes, xv–xvi, xx, 10, 143–162, 208
defined, xv–xvi, 10
inflections summarized, 208
Word groups, 106–112
Word lists (*see* Dolch; Fry; Single words; Word method; Word-by-word reading)
Word method, xvii–xviii, 5, 21–23, 38–39, 107–109, 119–120, 128, 133–142, 174–176, 183–184
Word order (*see* Sentence functions and function order)
"Word perception," 55
Word position (*see* Distribution)
Word structure (*see* Word-form changes)
Word use, 70, 145–147
Word-by-word reading, xvii–xviii, 5–6, 23, 44, 51, 55, 107, 112, 174–175, 183–184
(*See also* Single words; Word calling)
Written English, 195–196
Writing, viii, xix–xx, 4, 6–8, 15, 23, 39, 44, 52, 57, 60, 64–70, 75, 77–115, 117–133, 145–147, 151–162, 165–167, 175–177, 183–184, 191, 196
defined, 39, 165
Writing readiness defined, 39
(*See also* Graphic symbol system; Handwriting; Language arts instruction)